THIS IS HOW I FIGHT MY BATTLES

12 Ways To Win Against Your Giant

by
Nickalos T. Baker

Published by Watersprings Publishing, a division of
Watersprings Media House, LLC.
P.O. BOX 1284
Olive Branch, MS 38654
www.waterspringsmedia.com
Contact publisher for bulk orders and permission requests.

Copyrights © 2020 by Nickalos Baker

All rights reserved. No part of this publication may be reproduced, distributed, or transmitted in any form or by any means, including photocopying, recording, or other electronic or mechanical methods, without the prior written permission of the publisher, except in the case of brief quotations embodied in critical reviews and certain other noncommercial uses permitted by copyright law.

Scripture quotations credited to NIV are from the Holy Bible, New International Version. Copyright © 1973, 1978, 1984, 2011 by Biblica, Inc. Used by permission. All rights reserved worldwide.

Scripture quotations marked "ESV" are taken from The Holy Bible, English Standard Version. Copyright © 2000; 2001 by Crossway Bibles, a division of Good News Publishers. Used by permission. All rights reserved.

Printed in the United States of America.

Library of Congress Control Number: 2020904397

ISBN-13: 978-1-948877-44-2

TABLE OF CONTENTS

	Dedication	i
	Introduction	iii
Round 1	This Means War	2
Round 2	What Held Me, Could Not Hold Me	12
Round 3	Shackled Mentality	26
Round 4	Bruised but Not Broken!	37
Round 5	The Attack Was Sent to Elevate	43
Round 6	Which Way Should I Run?	48
Round 7	The Nature of Oppression	52
Round 8	Ignore the Invisible, Trust the Impossible	60
Round 9	Embrace the Impossible	66
Round 10	It's Your Time	71
Round 11	Today the Giant Falls	77
Round 12	We Will Win	83
	Summary and Conclusion	87
	About the Author	89

ACKNOWLEDGEMENTS

Where would I be had it not been for God's grace. I count it all joy through seasons of distress, through joy and sadness, it was meant for my good. This book is dedicated to my wife Tabatha, and our kids Angel, Nikayla, and Caleb, thank you for being patient as this book was being formulated and believing that it would be a great read. I would like to personally thank the Professors at Oakwood University for their scholarship, and the staff who served the Oakwood University Theology Department as I matriculated there from 2013-2015.

To my mentor, Dr. George Russell Seay, Jr., thank you for reassuring me that I was in the right place, in the right season, and that at the right time hard work would pay off. To the class of 2015, Corhort G, Vaughn Edmeade, Donald Monroe, my colleagues in ministry, coworkers, constituents, I want to say thank you for your support.

To my Mom and Dad for pouring into me much knowledge, as I was in pursuit of exploring ministry. Thanks, I couldn't have accomplished this milestone without you. To my uncle Clink for the ride back and forth to the revivals at South Park SDA Church many years ago. It was on the road traveling to and from revival that God gave me vision, and set me before ministry's door. I'm still cruising in my destiny.

Most importantly, I would like to thank the Lord. He is truly able to do exceedingly, abundantly above all I could ask of Him. The journey was challenging, but it was worth it. As a Servant Leader I stand, I represent along with you as we bring about the kind of revolution that our society has not seen in a long time. Through the portals of time and space we will lift the standard, we will leave our mark, we will change the world.

INTRODUCTION

If I told you that there was a way you could win every battle that came against you in this season, would you step in the ring? If I told you that the way to win your battles had everything to do with your determination and will to never lose again, would you believe it? What if I told you that the next attack against you is not necessarily an attack, but more of a lesson to prepare you for the fight against the greatest giant you will eventually face someday. Your Giant will show up. Giants come in different sizes, different shapes, and often with a plan to devour you. Be alarmed, but do not be dismayed. The One who is on your side is still undefeated. Jesus, the undefeated One is our friend and He will stick closer to us than any bother, no matter the fight.

Amazingly, in this season, this is How I Fight My Battles: 12 Ways to Win Against Your Giant makes a significant contribution to those who decide to take up their position, stand still, and see the salvation of the Lord. It is my belief that with intentional effort, prayer, and a battle strategy, you will celebrate great victories both now and later. I must admit, I had help against every giant that challenged me. After carefully observing little David fighting against Goliath his giant, I discovered that no matter the size of your giant, everyone one of them has a weak spot. In 1987, my parents bought a new Nintendo game for us, "Mike Tyson's Punch Out." The game had several rounds. In one of the rounds Little Mac had to defeat King Hippo. King Hippo would run up and lift his hand and make a sound attempting a knock-out punch. The only way Little Mac could defeat him was to hit him in the mouth. After that blow, the X or weak spot on King Hippo's stomach. Like Little Mac, find the weak spot on your spiritual giant. When the giant goes down it will never recover. What is your giant's weak spot? David's confidence is what found a weak spot in Goliath. If he could defeat his giant, you can too.

It was my first day of class in the MAPS program at Oakwood University in 2013. Dr. Harold Lee was my instructor. When he began to go over the syllabus, and told the class his expectations I said, "This is not for me, this is for the birds." It was my provision to leave and go home. However, I met two cool dudes that day, Vaughn Edmeade, who said "let's go to lunch", and I met motivational speaker Jeremy Anderson who took us. Listen, the very moment that I decided to throw in the towel regarding the MAPS program and head home, God had Jeremy Anderson near, and the brother began to speak life on our way to and from Newk's Eatery in Huntsville, AL.

Guess what? I thought I was average. Average won't cut it when you're on your way to the next level. Vaughn said it best, "Average is Failure." Indeed, before lunch I was ready to give up, but by the time Jeremy finished encouraging me that day, I was armed with more confidence believing I could accomplish anything, even getting through my class. After lunch I internally made a declaration to the syllabus in front of me, "this means war." When you face your giant, never forget that your TKO has everything to do with whose report you will believe.

Let's face it. There were times when we have all had high expectations for everybody but ourselves. We learned the hard way and that's ok. Know now that you are designed to be great, but greatness has everything to do with your will power and your belief that you can win. When it is your turn to make the difference, and the time has come, I hope you go for what you know. Know that you are more than a conqueror, and that you can do all things through Christ who gives you strength. In this season, go hard or go home!

On purpose there are moments when you will need to take a ring side seat against your giant. Choose your battles wisely. Resolution has always come out of a fight, so fight on. It is my hope as you read this book that you will stretch forth what you have. What you have is a hope and a future, and that God will bring you to an expected end. What do you expect? I expect to win. If you are ready to win, tell your giant, "Let's get ready to rumble!" With confidence say, "This is how I fight my Battles!"

ROUND 1
THIS MEANS WAR

It is obvious that as we live from day to day, we are faced with uncertainties in life, and we often deal with things that are beyond our control. No matter where we are in the world, who we are, whose we are, our background, gender, race, or creed, we do one of two things under present circumstances, we 'fight or flight'. Whenever things are going well some say, "I'm blessed." Whenever things are not so well, the same one's say, "I'm blessed." The truth of the matter is, you can be blessed, and still in a mess. You can have peace and joy and all the while not be truly happy at all. You can be courageous and fight, or you can be fearful and take flight, and be left with the reality of the worry of what you think you should have done. We lose sleep over what if's and maybe's, but I'm so glad that even with weary years and silent tears, in the present in times past, every revolution, whether spiritual, or physical, it has come out of a fight.

Fighting fair is a vague visual of what we often see. Whoever the judges are that score the points only see what's fair by the rules of their engagement, or simply by what they regard as fair depending on what they would think if they were on the other side of the attack. After you live for a while you will discover that every attack is not created equal. There are some attacks that elevate us and there are some attacks that diminish us. Some would have us question ourselves, all the while wondering whether or not we have won the fight.

Without further ado, please understand that balance is the key component to success. Do you know that the devil seeks to double his attacks against you to offset your balance? For this reason, we must turn up our praise, our devotion, and our prayers, if we know who's in control. Unapologetically, my praise will not, cannot, shall not be restricted, because I serve the CEO of the universe, He is God, He is not confined to a box. He is not confined to a temple made with hands. God is good and I don't have the right to remain silent. For the Bible says that the angels cry "Holy, holy, holy, is the Lord of hosts: the whole earth is full of His glory." He is God and there is no one like Him. Since a three-stranded cord is not easily broken, we can know that God is strong enough and mighty enough to handle the tough situations that come our way. When life seems unbearable, we are told to "look up." "And when these things begin to come to pass, then look up, and lift up your heads; for your redemption draweth nigh. " John 12:27-32 is the passage of scripture that we will use to construct the foundation for our spiritual reasoning. The other scriptures that we will use are just the windows and walls of the spiritual house. I plan to tear the house up, but only with the intention of building it up all over again.

Now is my soul troubled; and what shall I say? Father, save me from this hour: but for this cause came I unto this hour. Father, glorify thy name. Then came there a voice from heaven, saying, I have both glorified it, and will glorify it again. The people therefore, that stood by, and heard it, said that it thundered: others said, An angel spake to him. Jesus answered and said, This voice came not because of me, but for your sakes. Now is the judgment of this world: now shall the prince of this world be cast out. And I, if I be lifted up from the earth, will draw all men unto me.
John 12:27-32 KJV

In the early 80's, on Saturday nights we would recline at my grandparents' house and resolve to watch the Andy Griffith show. I shall never forget, on one-episode, little Opie was trying to convince little Sheldon why he could not give him a nickel to pass by his street, Opie told Sheldon that he could not give away his nickel because he owed it to his daddy.

Opie said "Besides, if I give it to you then how am I going to swallow my peanut butter and jelly sandwich without milk."

Sheldon said, "Opie give it up."

Then Opie said, "What if I don't want to."

Sheldon said, "Then that's a knuckle sandwich." So, Opie gave up his nickel. Sheldon said, "You better not tell anyone."

Opie said, "I know, cause then you will pulverize me, then you'll knock my block off, then hit me with the one-two, then jump on me." Opie went back, and his father figured it out by his trusty side kick, Barny. The father speaks to his son about one of his own experiences which led him to say to Opie, his giant, Sheldon, "Close your eyes, grit your teeth, take the punch, you won't feel a thing, after the punch, tear into him like a whirlwind." After Opie hears his father's words, he confronts the bully. Because of his Father's words, not only does Opie step across the street, he steps across the line that was drawn in the dirt by his giant. Opie gives Sheldon a good sucker punch, Sheldon falls, and his boys who were with him run away. Why? Because Opie is the man, he is lifted up, and his friends are drawn toward him.

What do you when faced with your giants? With the battle strategy given from the Father you will win. I guarantee it. Like Opie, I got into much trouble. With a family with one girl, and five boys, we had many wrestling matches ourselves. I learned that while fighting you should never tell a man what you are going to do to him before you do it, unless the victory is sure. Jesus has never lost a battle and it is fitting for Him to speak with confidence. Listen as Jesus speaks, "Now is the judgment of this world: now shall the prince of this world be cast out. And I, if I be lifted up from the earth, will draw all men unto me." If the Lord said it, you can count on it. Jesus knew that His earthly ministry was ending. He knew that He would face the Giant of death. He says to the disciples, "Verily, verily, I say unto you, except a corn of wheat fall into the ground and die, it abideth alone; but if it die, it bringeth forth much fruit." God has a plan. When our feet are planted in His will, we will not be uprooted. We were not built to be broken, nor created to be destroyed by the enemy. God has given us a plan, a purpose. Press on. Fight with perseverance. God has never lost a battle. For this reason, He will give you victory over the enemy, and power to pulverize him too.

In the gospel of John 12:20-24, Jesus ultimately wins the battle. Satan started the fight in heaven according to Revelation 12:7, and the fight then took a twisted turn, that's what serpents do. For the Bible declares, "There was a day when all the sons of God came to present themselves before the Lord, and Satan came also among them, And the Lord said, "Satan where have you come from, Satan said from roaming to and fro on the earth."

Now there was a day when the Sons of God came to present themselves before the Lord, and Satan came also among them. And the Lord said unto Satan, whence comest thou? Then Satan answered the Lord, and said, from going to and fro in the earth, and from walking up and down in it.
Job 1:6-7 KJV

Satan challenged God. Please note, if you are going to challenge God, challenge God, but don't challenge God in front of His boys. Satan is declaring that through the fall of Adam and Eve, that they are his subjects. Both of them decided to rebel against You, and they have sinned. Because of this, Adam lost his dominion, and Satan declares that he is the Prince of this world. If this was true, then why couldn't Satan take the book out of the hand of the One who sits on the throne? What's in the hand of Him that sits on the throne is the title deeds to the earth. Satan knows a lot, but he could not understand that it is the mingling of justice and mercy that establishes Gods throne. This is what crushed the serpents head prophetically looking at Genesis 3:15.

My battles cannot be compared to the controversy or battle between Christ and Satan, but I remember a similar incident all too well. True story. So, I am sitting in class and the bully of the class decided to pick on me. I'm so glad he did that day. Let's just say that it was his lucky day. I didn't talk much, because I was not one to waste words. The boy said something about my mama. I brushed the insult off, but then the boy said something about my "grandmama," and he said it in front of my boys. Now why would you say that? I asked myself and I answered with the assumption that he must want to fight. Well the right button got pushed that day, ding, ding, ding, the bells went off in my head, and a still small voice said "fight." I know it wasn't the Holy Spirit, but it sounded good, and it was one of the boys. I learned the hard way that just because something sounds good, perhaps even looks good, does not mean that it is good. I fought the bully, but that's not all that happened. In the office, we were both paddled. The principal is the one who one that fight.

If the controversy between Christ and Satan was a boxing match it would go this way. "In the blue corner stands the boxer by the name of Lucifer, aka Satan, the wise serpent of old, with dragon speed who growls, and prowls and roars like a lion, he is wearing every precious stone for his covering. His hometown, heaven, the pre-fight record by way of knock out, 1 and 0, Weight, is enough to beset any man or woman. Height, is SIX, SIX, SIX. Style, he sealest up the sum, full of wisdom and beauty, cunning, deceiving, wild and unorthodox. Recognition, he is disputed heavyweight champion of this world.

In the red corner stands the boxer named Jesus, also known as the Good Shepherd, the Son of God, Son of Man, the Bread of Life, the Vine, the Lamb, the High Priest, the Lord, King, the Savior, the I AM. He is wearing a long white robe, soiled in His own blood. His hometown, is heaven, but also Earth, by way of Bethlehem. The pre-fight record by way of knock out. Who knows, "For the secret things belong to God, but the things revealed belong to us." Weight, is unknown as the Alpha and Omega. Height, is inexpressible, but incredible. Style, is of no reputation, as he was wounded, pierced, humbled, and obedient to death, even death on a cross. For the hour has come and I'm Ready. The Referee says to Jesus and to Satan, this is the fight that the world has been waiting to see, billions upon trillions are watching, the rules are applied in the ring, just as they were in the dressing room. Protect yourself at all times, go to your corners." So Jesus goes to Gethsemane, Satan goes to Annas and Caiaphas, which led him to Pontius Pilate who said, I find no fault in Him.

The Source of God's power is bigger than the strength of my opponent.

When we focus on the power of God more than the strength of our opponent, we will come out victorious. How do I know? For example, Luke 8:34-48 tell us about the woman with the issue of blood who pressed her way toward Jesus. Her faith at work set her up to press her way. She left that experience with a blessing. With great will, she probably said within herself, " Devil you won't win today, somebody got to go down, and I refuse to be counted out." The source of God's power, was bigger than the strength of her opponent.

I must confess and tell you that great things never come from comfort zones, get in the fight. Satan flexed his muscles, grunted, and raved about his soon to have victory. What Satan did not know this time, was that the victory would not come by way of who is left standing, but by way of who falls to the ground. God kept His cool because He knew that the fight was fixed. He is from everlasting to everlasting. God is in control and He cannot fail. If in Christ we ever lose, it was because there was going to be victory in our defeat. There can only be one winner. Jesus is the One.

How many of us know today, that The LORD will fight for you? But understand this, sometimes you got to learn how to be still. As the lord fights for you, you have to learn how to keep your cool through praising God, praying, and meditating on the word. We've got to learn how to focus on the power of God rather than the strength of our opponent. I hope that you are excited just to know that The LORD is your light and your salvation whom shall we fear? The LORD is the stronghold of your life of whom shall you be afraid?"

Six days before the Passover, Jesus goes to Bethany to be with His friends for His farewell visit. While there, His head and feet are anointed, and for that reason He is ultimately disrespected by the haters who showed up. So Jesus makes His way to Jerusalem (Luke 19:28-44). Jesus chose a donkey at that moment. Those who were hating on Him that day would ultimately see Him later, riding on a white horse (Revelation

11:19). See what Kings do! See Jesus riding into town on that donkey, see the disciples giving each other high fives as the people declare their Hosannas, and saying, "Blessed is he who comes in the name of the Lord."

They cried their loud hosannas, blessed is He who comes in the name of the Lord, they knew who He was on Sunday, but on Friday they would rather have Barabbas instead.

Therefore, what Jesus had on His mind was His mission, so he spoke in a parable. Jesus used a parable to display and demonstrate how His mission should be accomplished. John 12:24 states, "Unless a corn of wheat falls into the ground, and die, it abideth alone: but if it dies, it bringeth forth much fruit." Jesus is speaking to His disciples with the reality that the Passover was near, and again because Lazarus was raised from the dead, the fame of Christ had been scattered abroad. All of a sudden, some Greeks showed up and said to Philip, we would see Jesus, (John 12:20-21). What made these Greeks distinguished, is the reality that they were not like your nominal church goers. Most of the people who were present at the temple were in touch with the Church, but they were out of touch with Jesus. Jesus concludes in His mind, if the Greeks are coming to see Me, then it's time for the Son of Man to be glorified. With this being said, how can you know that your church or business is on the right track? Well, you will know that your church is on the right track when folks from the outside, come looking on the inside for the Jesus you make famous. Making Jesus famous does not come by way of you sitting down, get out there and tell somebody that the battle has been won. This is how I fight my battles.

Conspiracy theorists think they can prove that the Floyd Mayweather-Danny Pacquiao fight was fixed. The judges made some errors, but in John 12 The Righteous Judge makes no mistakes, He knows how to watch the clock, and He knows how to adjust the thermostat of your bout. The heavenly Father glorified your name by turning up the heat, and I will glorify it again, He states. Jesus said, "in this life you would have trouble but keep your peace because he has already overcome the world."

John 12 sums it all up. The fight is fixed, and the outcome is already determined. Friends we are just going through the motions, and some will lose against their giant of addiction, giant of pride, giant of gossiping, giant of insecurities, but let it not be so with you.

The elders, the chief priests, and the scribes where representatives of those who were filled up with everything, except for the right things, and for this reason Jesus couldn't do anything with them. But if we are honest with ourselves, we get bogged down on the spiritual journey because we sometimes are so busy pouring into ourselves stuff we don't need. And the reason why some of us can't praise Him right now as we hang with Jesus, can't praise in our trial, won't praise Him during our test, won't praise Him even in the good times nor the bad, is because we have been so comfortable running on empty. Running on empty is not all bad, at least if we run out, God can fill us up.

As Christians, often we get slapped by the waves of broken and unaccomplished dreams. We wonder sometimes, Lord, "How did I get here!" I'd rather hang with Jesus, in my pain, in my storm, no release, my captivity, I'll hang with You God because I know You are up to something. God is trying to anchor us deep. (Max Lucado). Sometimes, our need to be comfortable has become our own prison. Remember, unless a corn of wheat falls to the ground, it abides alone, but if it dies it will bring forth much fruit (John 12:24). The resurrection is sown in corruption, but raised in incorruption, it is sown in dishonor, it is raised in glory, it is sown in weakness, but raised in power.

I stopped by here to tell somebody, despite whatever you go through in this life, God knows the beginning and the end. When you are in Christ you must come to the place where you are content. In this life, I discovered that you just simply got to be ready for anything, anywhere, your giant will show up. With the Word of God, you can win your battles.

Don't let your past have power over your right now experience.

Jesus was not the only one in that ring, there were two thieves on the Cross who needed an encounter with the eternal. An encounter with the Savior. We need an encounter today by coming to grips with who we are so that we can see what it is we need to change. I came to declare by the power of the Holy Spirit that there needs to be some confession, there needs to be some cleansing, there needs to be some removal of anger and hatred so we can see Jesus. God selected you because He was trying to set you up for blessings, but sometimes, God must withhold the blessings because we handcuff Him by our unwillingness to make the lifestyle changes that are consistent with God's design. When Jesus said, Father forgive them for they know not what they do. Both thieves on the cross had the promise of God, while one found himself clinging to the set-back of the self-inflicted curse of his past. The other one decides not to let what happened in his past have power over what Jesus was trying to do in his right now. Had you not been set back, had you not been in trouble, had you not been released from your last job, had you not been exposed to your storm, you would have not known that God was going to provide you with the umbrella of His majesty. The source of His strength is better than the sting of my circumstance.

Don't become an outsider because you have no inner relationship with God.

What I have discovered is that you don't get to choose how you find Christ, but you get to choose how you follow Him. In other words, don't be found guilty of being influenced by your culture, rather than by your Christ. The culture said you were not good enough.

It was a mind thing, whoever or whatever controls your mind controls you. We want to be saved, we want to be transformed, but we don't want to be stretched. God is saying to us, don't expect to get through new doors with old keys. We want the Lord to do new things in us, but don't want to break old habits. Let's look to the Lord. He is the source of our strength.

Don't let your mind keep you from divine revelation of who Jesus is.

Some suggest that Muhammad Ali was the greatest boxer who ever lived. He was the greatest boxer who died. The greatest boxer who ever lived was Jesus. What made Muhammad Ali the greatest, was not because he was the strongest, or the fastest, or his ability to float like a butterfly and sting like a bee. What made him the greatest was his belief that he was. Jesus was not the best looking, nor the best groomed, was not the richest, but what makes Him my Savior, is that while I was a sinner, He died for me, and when He could've said no, He said yes. When He should have declared, Father consume them, He said Father forgive them. "In my preaching voice" Is there anybody reading this who's glad that while we were messed up, Jesus showed up, and because Jesus showed up, the enemy's plan was interrupted. Gabriel the Angel had pointed up at all those who would go up (Heaven), it had fixed an opportunity for Jesus to say, "If I be lifted up, I'll draw all men unto me." John 12:32 KJV. I am healed because of His stripes. Somebody may be in need of healing today, somebody may be in need of deliverance today, somebody may be in need of some joy right now, you might not even deserve it, but you have made up in your mind by faith, you are going to get it. Hey, if you're anything like me, if it doesn't come soon enough, you don't mind praising God while you wait.

They taunted Jesus. Who? Soldiers, family members, haters, the church, councilmen and councilwomen? Their words, "If you be the King of the Jews come down off that cross." The reason why he didn't come down is because He was more than just a King. He is Lord, and Savior. It wasn't the nails that held Him to that cross. Check this out. Behind His blood-stained hands, and that plank of wood was the catalogue of my sins. He covered me, and He covered you, He kept us when we couldn't keep ourselves.

It was necessary that you lost your mind, so that His mind could be in you. It was necessary that you lost your way, so that He could have His way. It was necessary for you to throw in the towel, because it was only until you made Jesus your last resort that He was going to step in and deliver you. He stopped dying to Save a sinner like me.

Great things never come from comfort zones, get in the fight.

Reflections

1. Have you ever been under attack? What is your winning strategy? Remember, whatever controls your mind controls you.

ROUND 2
WHAT HELD ME, COULD NOT HOLD ME

Notes from a traumatized prophet
Habakkuk 1:2-4, 5-6, 12

Habakkuk's First Complaint, *Habakkuk 1:2-4,*

How long, Lord, must I call for help, but you do not listen? Or cry out to you, "Violence!" but you do not save? Why do you make me look at injustice? Why do you tolerate wrongdoing? Destruction and violence are before me; there is strife, and conflict abounds. Therefore the law is paralyzed, and justice never prevails. The wicked hem in the righteous, so that justice is perverted.

The Lord's Answer, *Habakkuk 1:5-6*

"Look at the nations and watch and be utterly amazed. For I am going to do something in your days that you would not believe, even if you were told. I am raising up the Babylonians, that ruthless and impetuous people, who sweep across the whole earth to seize dwellings not their own.

Habakkuk's Second Complaint, *Habakkuk 1:12*

Lord, are you not from everlasting? My God, my Holy One, you will never die. You, Lord, have appointed them to execute judgment; you, my Rock, have ordained them to punish. Your eyes are too pure to look on evil; you cannot tolerate wrongdoing. Why then do you tolerate the treacherous? Why are you silent while the wicked swallow up those more righteous than themselves?

Habakkuk's Third Complaint, *Habakkuk 2:1*

I will stand at my watch and station myself on the ramparts; I will look to see what he will say to me, and what answer I am to give to this complaint.

The Lord's Answer, *Habakkuk 2:2-3*

Then the Lord replied: "Write down the revelation and make it plain on tablets so that a herald may run with it. For the revelation awaits an appointed time; it speaks of the end and will not prove false. Though it linger, wait for it; it will certainly come and will not delay."

Put on your seatbelt folks, Habakkuk is about to take you on an adventurous ride. What we go through in life sometimes doesn't make sense. That's how we feel. God is trying to change the way we see things. Have you ever called on God when you had a problem, and it seemed as if the problem intensified? Don't make sense. Check this out.

The name Habakkuk means: "The cordially embraced one (favorite of God), or the cordial embracer." Wrestler

Some scholars suggest that Habakkuk lived in Judah toward the end of Josiah's reign (640-609 B.C.) or at the beginning of Jehoiakim's reign (609-598). It contains, rather, a dialogue between the prophet and God. He is not a major prophet, but he has something to say.

I am sick of this!

See, what was happening in the moment when Habakkuk did not understand why he was having challenges, God was just giving a process that was already in motion before the foundation of the world was ever created. Habakkuk found himself in a situation and did not realize that his situation was orchestrated by God to bring God's people (slavery) to a place where they would know that God is their King, and that He is in control. Habakkuk was one like myself, who loved to state, "If it is not consistent with my purpose, my destiny, I don't want it." But if the truth be known, that which we don't desire may just be what we need to have our faith exercised to get us to our destination.

God puts things in your life, then remove the thing in your life because He wants you to depend on Him, not the thing.

Why is Habakkuk not satisfied at this juncture? Why is this assignment God has given so difficult to handle?

Maybe Habakkuk is upset because he believes that if you are chosen by God, then you should always know what God is doing. News Flash, if you got to know what God is always doing, you will never be satisfied, and you will never have any peace. Why? Because a lot of stuff that God does, don't make sense. God's ways are not our ways, His thoughts, are higher than ours. No wonder why the secret things belong to Him, and things revealed belong to us.

Let's face it, if God showed us everything we would go through, I'm afraid, that we would run from God rather than run to Him. If the truth be told, sometimes culture, customs, conventions, even traditions, and what we think get in the way of progress, and what God is trying to do.

True Story, I was walking to my Grandparents house after school one day and a big dog was tied to a tree near someone's home. I had on my brand new white Reeboks, and I was busy being cool after school. For me, East Highland Middle school brings back many memories. On this particular day, my boys: Carlos, Quinton, and Jamel were walking home after school when we noticed that the big dog was not in the same area as usual, nor on the chain. Well, if there is anything I could do professionally, it was running, at least from dogs. I ran, fell, jumped, and never broke my stride, but I got scars I tell you.

Guess what? I have scars, and you have scars too. In fact, all God's children have scars. If we are not careful, we will find ourselves tangled up, mangled up, or even caught up in the net of other people's thoughts of us. The apostle Paul states, "From henceforth let no man trouble me: for I bear in my body the marks of the Lord Jesus."

That's why I come today with no colonized gospel that would have you to sit on the sidelines, and spectate on yesterday and today's injustices. But a revolutionized Gospel, not driven by a Eurocentric Christ, but by a Radical Lord who bled and died, that will not afford you to remain silent. Perhaps, the reason why we fall victim to the atrocities that we face is because we have bought into the perception that a promise received, should be void of pain. The prophet Habakkuk is traumatized because he did not understand that the enslavement of his people should fit into the plan of a God who is loving, passionate, and in total control. The same lesson God was giving to Habakkuk; is the same lesson the Lord is teaching us. Here it is, slavery was just part of God's plan to unveil His will in motion, to show us that what happened over 400 years ago, ought to inform us that over 2000 years ago, somebody received a name above every name, and that name given, confirms the unveiling of something already in motion before the foundations of the world.

Habakkuk found himself in a situation and did not realize that it was orchestrated by God to bring him, and them, into a place where they would know that God is there King, and that God is in control. That's why your praise should not, cannot, shall not be restricted if you know you serve the CEO of the universe. He is God. He is not confined to a box. He is not confined to a temple made with hands. The prophet Isaiah saw the Lord High and lifted up. The robe of His trained filled the temple." He is God and there is no one like Him. Because I'm in the presence of the Lord, I can lift up my hands in the struggle, I lift up my heart while in despair, and I can lift up my head, because my redemption is drawing near.

Would you know that God can put things in your life, then remove the thing out of your life because He wants you to be dependent upon Him, and not the thing. We still trip up over things that God has already resolved, but it's hard to change your mind and at the same time be renewed by your own reality. Note: Just because folks think they are ahead of you, don't mean that they are above you. While we focus on what others say about us, the devil is gaining ground. We get mad, we put our religion down. You are waiting on God to show up, but God is waiting on you to grow up. Habakkuk, stop complaining and start confirming what God has said. Habakkuk believed that God's people would be wiped out, because he had forgotten about the promise. I am persuaded, that sometimes you got to go through some stuff, so that you can embrace what God is trying to do.

The reason why you are under attack is because God is getting ready to maneuver you into the next level of your blessing. The attack has come because the devil stands in opposition to the declining progress he's had on your life, and he knows that this is a now or never moment. The devil knows that if you step into your next dimension, that the battle is over. The battle is over because the attack was sent and set up by God to elevate you. The elevation is not so much as status, but a raising of something, or someone into a higher place. That place is in the presence of the Lord. Write the vision because something is about to happen.

Habakkuk is writing because he is trying to convey to us that sometimes you got to wait for your promise, and when it shows up it shall speak and not lie.

Just like Habakkuk, your enslavement, and entrapment was sent by God, so that when it happened, it would arouse His Holy anger, so that He could ultimately move the enemy out of the way and make a way by preparing you for the promise, and the coming of His Son.

I think now would be a good time to bring another witness in on this promise. Somebody who not only ministers to our physical need, our emotional need, and our spiritual need. Maybe the apostle Luke can testify to what he has seen and heard. Luke was not an eye witness, but he writes what he hears, and he writes so that people who find themselves traumatized like Habakkuk would know that your connectedness to God does not take away you being a candidate for suffering. Luke would tell you that in order for you to get some notoriety, you will go through some obscurity. When Luke writes, he writes so that you would know that just because you're in the background, doesn't mean that you won't be brought to the forefront.

You can be a prophet, you can be an apostle, you can be a Prince of royalty on one day, and on the next day be snatched into a dry place. You can be the crowning work of God's creation, and at the same time feeling you are about to die. Some are wondering, how can I be chosen and at the same time under attack? How can I be chosen and lose this job because of people who have a problem with the pronunciation of my first name? How can I be chosen and have to bury this child? How can I be chosen but still get cancer? How can I be chosen and have my family stripped away, how can I be chosen and end up in slavery and captivity? What good is it to be chosen if I got to go through all of this? If you live long enough you will come to discover, that God will make sense out of stuff that don't make sense. It's a setup.

Have you ever been held by or up by something or someone who tried to keep you from getting where you were trying to go? Have you ever been stuck in a storm, and where you were kept you from getting to your destination? If you live long enough you will discover that it is very difficult to go where you want to go, when the devil has gained much of your territory. From Genesis to Revelation you know that the devil, who has claimed much of your territory, suggesting that he walks to and from through it and on it, is not in control of it at all. God is a moving God. Because God is moving God, He transitions us through different places, and phases. The reason why He transitions us is so that we won't become comfortable where we are.

Through American history some suggest that 1619 is the year that slaves were transported from Africa to Virginia. However, 1619 is not the best place to start with African people in America. In the 1500's the Negroes who were enslaved and plundered by Sir Francis Drake were already at work near present day South Carolina, 1619 attempts to dismiss the memory of the oceans floor, death, and the Atlantic Slave trade.

To this day, according to Jasper Copping, the quest for the sunken slave ship which claimed 664 lives has never been found. While that may be exciting news for some, there is still the reality that the smallest number that can be counted of all the African men women and children who died in the middle passage was at least 9 million, at the bottom of the sea. As the slave ship called Leusden was laden with human cargo, as she sank into the murky depths, the captain ordered his crew to send the slaves below deck and for the hatches to be nailed shut to keep them there. It is a fact, that in order for a ship to go down, something from the outside had to come over into it.

I suggest that we are living in a time where the 'Fake News' on the outside should not get rid of the good news on the inside. Learn how to keep stuff on the outside on the outside, that way, when you are going through it, it won't go through you.

The places God uses for greatness start from low places.

In order for you to experience greatness, sometimes you have to do what you don't want to do to get where you want to be. At UPS on the sorting isle, we could not choose what type of packages that would come down the slide, but when they came down, we could only choose what to do with them. How did we know what to do with the packages? We only knew what to do with the packages by the label that was on them.

Joseph had a label on him. He was hated by his brothers because of the coat that he possessed was colorful. I've lived long enough to know that your colorfulness can land you in a place of brokenness. My colorfulness is the cleverness of what God would use to place me where He wanted me to be.

Joseph was thrown into a pit by those he loved. Sometimes the only way God can launch you into the next level is by taking you, tossing you, or towing you into some deep stuff, some low places. Joseph was thrown into a pit, but the pit was just a set up for the palace.

Daniel was thrown into the Lion's Den by a decree because of those who conspired against him, but in his low place is where the Angel of the Lord showed up. The same thing that the enemy tried to use against you, God flipped the script for you to use against them. I'm so glad that while the devil had me messed up, somebody showed up, I suggest that it was the Lord, all the glory belongs to Him.

Jesus stepped out of Glory, left the praise and adoration of the angels, left His Father's side, pressed through the portals of time and space. He is the Word, and the Word became flesh, in Him is life and the life is the light of us who can conclude, that the reason our Savior was born in a barn is because the places that God uses for greatness, start from low places.

Statistics say racial bias keeps more people of color in prisons and on probation than ever before. One out of three black boys, one out of three Latino boys, compared with one out of every 17 white boys born today can expect to go to prison in his lifetime. Mnay may stay there because of the excessive sentences given through intentional sanctions that would never lift us up, but annihilate, decimate, and exterminate us until we have been bruised, battered and beaten down into a low place. But my low place was just a set up for what God is getting ready to do.

Revolution has always come out of a fight, but it's hard to fight when all odds are stacked against you. That's why you have to keep fighting. The day you stop fighting is the day you start dying. Because self-reliance is insufficient, we need divine intervention, especially in the court of law.

The plaintiff in a court case is the person who has filed a complaint-charges against the defendant for prosecution by the courts, while the defendant is the person who is refuting the charges and is seeking to prove their innocence. The justice system is corrupt, and somebody's elusive tradition, and fake news to "make America great Again," makes them think that they have ascended above the stars of God and the heights of the clouds. What goes up, will come down. Let's humble ourselves under the mighty hand of God, because the places that God uses for greatness come from low places.

Your attitude can determine your altitude.

When you are on the outside looking in, it is easy to pass judgment on others when you can't hear what's going on. Sometimes it takes someone from the outside to see and hear what's going on so that you can know that there is a different perspective than yours. There is nothing wrong with being different, there is nothing wrong with change. There will always be opposition, and the opposition needs to be embraced. Why? Because in it we can see people for who they really are, no disguising when one disagrees. I would like to suggest that it is a mind thing. So often we have high expectations for everyone but ourselves. We were designed to be great, but greatness has everything to do with your will power and your belief to press forward. There is a nature to your oppression, and the only way you can see it sometimes is by getting away from it, to observe it, so that you can call it what it is. When you discover it, make it your business to respond by saying, "If it is not consistent with my purpose, and my destiny, I don't want it." When all you know and all you hear are seeds of doubt, that you are not worth it, you got to go to a higher place so that you can see and hear what God wants you to do. What God wants you to do is let nobody turn you around.

Eleanor Roosevelt states, "No one can make you feel inferior without your consent." She was also quoted in saying, "The purpose of life is to live it, to taste experience to the utmost, to reach out eagerly and without fear for newer and richer experiences." That sounds good, but don't mean nothing to people who had to endure some shackles, and chains. For I am convinced right now, that God's people, in such a time as this, know that there is no one like Jesus. When He speaks, because of the Spirit of the living God now residing in you, you can find yourself in a terrifying position, and still consider it done. When He commands we can recognize that it stood fast. Jesus, when I look into the mirror I see how He was able to take nothing and make something out of it. The haters have said, "You would never be nothing, and that you look like nothing, and you are going nowhere, all you got is a little potential." But I'm so glad today, that when God looks at me, He does not see my present reality, He sees my future potential. Tell the devil who cares about your thought process and your assessment about me, I didn't ask you, so why you trying to remind me of the past when God has said, He has plans to prosper me in my future (Jeremiah 29:11). I know where my help comes from, my help comes from the Lord. For this reason, I will not keep silent!

I serve you notice today that just because you watched the movie 12 years a Slave, Rosewood, and Roots don't mean that you have seen the totality of the brutality of what I have been through. If God is in it, I'm thinking now. If God was in this and He was, then the attack against me, was sent, not to injure me, not to impair me, but to improve me. If God was in my mess, in my captivity, then the attack against me was sent, not to annihilate me, not to eradicate me, but to validate that I am somebody. And no matter where I go, no matter where I'm transported from, no chain can hold me down. I shall reign victorious. If God is in it, then the attack against me, was sent, not to hurt me, but to help me. If you think you got it bad.

The Bible says in Acts 2:23-24 of Jesus of Nazareth, "This man was handed over to you by God's deliberate plan and foreknowledge; and you, with the help of wicked men, put him to death by nailing him to the cross. 24 But God, raised him from the dead, freeing him from the agony of death, because it was impossible for death to keep its hold on him." The reason why I had to go through what I went through, was so that I could go through. Jesus did not just show up and give His life because it was the Fathers deliberate plan. Before the foundation of the world Jesus is the lamb that was slain. Jesus understood that there was a reward on the other side of the cross. And because He was obedient to death, He has been given a name above every name. So, my enslavement then, my captivity, is the portal of entry God uses to get me to the next stage in my life. The attack was just a gift, and the gift was designed and deliberated by God, to elevate me from my low place.

The reason why so many of us don't rise above our problems, historical facts, and shackled mentalities is because sometimes we focus so much on what we see, that we don't remember the good things that we heard. God has to setup situations that we don't like, that we don't want to experience, just for us to have faith. We walk by faith, and not by sight. Don't get side tracked or discouraged by what you see, shift your focus on what you have heard. What have you seen? What have you heard?

Well, I've been around for a while, I've seen the whites only and blacks only signs, I've seen some lynching's, I've seen some floggings, I've seen some marching, I've seen some protesting, I've seen some suffering, but what I was seeing cannot be compared to the glory of that which I heard. For the Bible says in Isaiah 54:17, "No weapon formed against me shall prosper and that every tongue that rises against me shall be condemned." What have you seen? I've seen some injustice, I've seen killings of unarmed colored folks, I've seen some mass incarceration and the New Jim Crow, I've seen some voter suppression, and even a nailing to a cross, but what I've seen cannot be compared to the glory that shall be revealed, and to the glory of what I heard.

I don't know anyone or anything that likes to be confined or caged in unless it's for the purpose of their protection. For example, the natural habitat for the lion is nature, not a cage. If the lion is caged in, it will rebel and fight because it's not content, but if the truth be told there are some spiritual incarcerations, and some shackled mentalities that have developed among us, because of what has been imposed on us. The lion that's caged is at the mercy of the one who put it there. Have you ever felt boxed in? I'm so glad to inform you today, that if you feel boxed in by what has been imposed on you, that you are not at the mercy of the those who put you there. You might have been in chains, but the chains were only a holding tool for God to do His marvelous work. There are those who fought to have equal rights, while others declare that all men are created equal, and endowed by their creator, but yet at the same time suggest that black slaves were 3/5 of a human. Yes, times have changed, seasons have changed, but mindsets remain. We are living in a time where dreamers are discouraged to dream.

Some suggest that we have been set free by decrees. We celebrate our independence, emancipation, and amendments. These things are good, but I want to let you know that I have been blood-washed, set free, it has been signed sealed and delivered in the courts above. Why? Because what held me could not hold me. What they said about you might have held you, it might have hurt you. What was done might have shackled you, but what held you could not hold you. According to John 1:10, Jesus was in the world and the world new Him not, He came to His own and His own received Him not. The Bible states, "Fellow

Israelites, listen to this: Jesus of Nazareth was a man accredited by God to you by miracles, wonders and signs, which God did among you through him, as you yourselves know. I was handed over to you by God's deliberate plan and foreknowledge; and you, with the help of wicked men, put him to death by nailing him to the cross. But God, raised him from the dead, freeing him from the agony of death." Why? Because it was impossible for death to keep its hold on me.

I'm glad to inform you today that what held me could not hold me. Is there anybody here who's glad that what held you could not hold you? If so, then give God a praise.

The same God who had the power to prevail in the beginning is the same God who has the power to prevail right now. If you trust in the Lord, He will make sense of what it is that you go through.

If it's not enough for you to know that the places that God uses come from low places, then maybe it's enough for you to know that the shift in your attitude, can change your altitude. If it's not enough for you to know that if you shift your attitude, you can change your altitude, then maybe it would be enough for you to know that what held you could not hold you. The Bible says, that whom the son sets free, is free indeed. I Am free.

When God has given you a vision, a purpose, and a plan, act on it.

Reflections

1. What's holding you back from your destiny?
   Can you think of anything that is keeping you from your goals, dreams, and aspirations?

2. What are you going to do about it?

ROUND 3
SHACKLED MENTALITY

When you fear failing more than you fear moving forward to progression, you remain where you are, shackled in a state of fear and uncertainty. "I'm Good." That is a slogan that is highly used today, but most of the time it is said, there is some hurt or attitude behind it, and it cannot be hidden. There are some things in life that you cannot afford to brush off or play way. It was a great day, and a sad day at the same time. The decree had gone forth to free the slaves, some were so used to the lifestyle of being a slave, that they developed a slave mentality. Remember this, the slave mentality keeps us where we are, and deters us from where we should go.

I see it clearly now, why some of the African slaves who were harshly treated if you will, remained on the slave plantation versus hitting the road or even making a break for freedom. It was because of their fear of uncertainty. For many it wasn't their thoughts of being scourged, if they tried to leave, after all, getting whipped, or flogged, raped, or castrated was painful, but that was their normal in their current society. The reality of feeling inferior, hopeless, homeless, meaningless, with nowhere to go, kept many of them stagnant and stuck. But today is a new day, a new era, a new dawning. Unfortunately, both men and women of color had been taking orders for over 400 years. However, because of a miraculous shift, and a Sovereign God who has spoken up, and has closed up slavery's doors, injustice will no longer reign victorious over those who were once bound. Why? For this hour I have now come, speak up! We don't have the right to keep silent. In fact, we will give order by our right to assemble peacefully and protest. Some people are okay with their present circumstance, but most of us are striving to become better, to experience more, to accept challenges when they rise because we know that out of pain, we gain. Revolution has always come out of some fight. Have you ever wondered why people who have the opportunity to make progressive steps, to make a positive impact for themselves and others choose not to do so?

If it is not consistent with my purpose, my destiny, I don't want it.

Time out. No longer should you wrestle in your head with worry of the rhetoric said about you. When we become comfortable with other people's thoughts and opinions of us, we will sell ourselves short trying to please everybody else. Here is a question for you. Are you ready? Have you ever seen progress by pleasing everyone else? I hope not. It's time to face the facts. Everyone will not like your decisions, nor your methods. Some people have a problem with giving you the credit you deserve. My advice, don't worry about them, they have a shackled mentality. There is nothing wrong with being different, there is nothing wrong with change, but what we can't change is the color of our skin. Can an Ethiopian change his color? Can a leopard change his spots? God made us the way He wanted us to be. There will always be opposition, and the opposition needs to be embraced. Why? Because, in it we can see people for who they really are, no disguising when one disagrees. I would like to suggest that it is a mind thing. So often we have high expectations for everybody but ourselves. We were designed to be great, but greatness has everything to do with your will-power and your belief to press forward. When it is your turn to make the difference, and the time has come, will you stand? There is a nature to your oppression, and the only way you can see it sometimes is by getting away from it, to observe it, so that you can call it what it is. When you discover it make it your business to respond by saying, "If it is not consistent with my purpose, my destiny, I don't want it."

For a long time, I was unaware that the reason why I had fallen behind in several things I wanted to accomplish did not come by way of what somebody else was willing to give me, but had everything to do with my own determination to accomplish what I desired. What I'm suggesting to you right now is that sometimes self is the only one stopping potential. It's time to make a believer out of your own self. Have you ever been told that you have good potential? Joshua, one of my younger brothers told me in a conversation that I had good potential. He probably doesn't remember the conversation, but I do. We were discussing life goals and I was sharing with him my intentions to pursue pastoral ministry at the time, mind you this was in 2010 six years before I got a call to serve as pastor in the South Central-Conference of SDA. By the way, when my brother said to me I had good potential, I wanted to convey that I had more than potential, I had a dream, and God also had a plan.

Like me, I'm sure that the best way you could express how you may have felt in similar circumstances, is by showing them versus telling them. When God has given you a dream, you can't wait around to see how the assignment will come to you, or what others think of you. Go pursue it, set goals, do your fair share by operating with intentional work, and faith. When God has given you a vision, a purpose, and a plan, act on it. Don't try to analyze it or figure it out, trust God, because He has it already worked out. Don't settle for where you are, "Average is Failure."

"Average is failure."
-Vaughn Edmeade

I wasn't called to be compared.
-Bishop Noel Jones

There is confirmation of my transformation. (Mark 5:1-20) You will not be the same! - God is saying to us, "I sanctified you before you were born, before your mother gave you your name, I ordered your steps, nobody knew you but me, (Jeremiah 1:5). I destined you for greatness, what are you doing here, in this place of darkness, in trouble, in chains. Why are you stuck when nothing now is holding you or keeping you except your imagination of what folks think, and what folks did in the past to you. You weren't called to be compared. Step out let me see you, come out so I can deal with the opposition at hand. The source of God's power is greater than the strength of our opponent. You are significant, and the proof of it is tied up in what you have been through. Your cloudy days, and your hills to climb, your test, your storm, your captivity, your attack was all tailor made so that when God brought you out, you would recognize that you are somebody.

The devil wanted to keep you where you were, he wanted to isolate you and get you all alone, away from your family and friends, away from those who love you, hoping that they would just pass by. But it isn't happening with the King of Kings and Lord of Lords. Call out to Him, run to Him, and worship Him. God knew what He was about to do in your life, that's why you were under attack, it was His reason to show up. Without the attack you would have never called, but because He loves you, He showed up. Maybe this is the same demon possessed man in chapter 5, this may be the same possessed man in Mark Ch. 1. If the devil can't get you in the street, he will get you in the church. He will bring the fight to you. Why? He believes he is in control. (Job 1:6) In Mark 1:21-24, Jesus called for the unclean spirit to come out, but Luke 11:24-26 states, "When the unclean spirit is gone out of a man, he walketh through dry places, seeking rest; and finding none, he saith, I will return unto my house whence I came out. And when he cometh, he findeth it swept and garnished. Then goeth he, and taketh to him seven other spirits more wicked than himself; and they enter in, and dwell there: and the last state of that man is worse than the first."

Immediately, when Jesus got out of the boat, the man ran toward Jesus and worshipped Him. Who was worshipping, the man or the demon. The demon caused the man to run, but the worship was just a disguise. I come to let somebody know today that you can't trick Jesus. Those who worship Him, must worship Him not only in spirit, but also in truth (John 4:24). Please note that this demon ran to church, ran to bible study, ran to worship, and even ran to Jesus. Moving forward is always the first step, but if we are going to be delivered and set free from what binds us, it's by our willingness to be changed. Maybe the reason the man who was possessed by the devil could not leave from the tombs for these reasons. Maybe he was embarrassed. Maybe the hatred of others had caused the warmth of his love to turn cold. Maybe he could not leave from where he was because he was so busy fighting himself. Perhaps he didn't get the promotion. Maybe he didn't make the team. Under the control of Satan, the demoniac now only expresses himself through self-inflicting wounds, self-inflicted trials, self-inflicted pain, self-inflicted suffering.

It's hard to fight against the stuff that makes us feel good, and look good, comfortable and content where we are, but if the truth be told, sometimes we be in a mess. The devil knows that in our own strength we are no match for him, but if we submit to God, and have faith, he is defeated. The demoniac in Mark Ch. 5 was fighting, yelling, and crying out because of his torment. This is what happens physically, mentally, and spiritually for those who are captive by the enemy. I was a captive. I was a slave to sin entangled in mess that I made for myself, but I'm glad that Jesus came among the mental tomb in my life. It does not matter how dark your midnight; Jesus will show up. He found me where I was and set me free. For that reason, I can shout. Holler if you hear me. Praise God. He is in the business of showing up. When God shows up, do not be alarmed at Him asking, "What is your name?" Question, why would the all-wise God, all-knowing God, omniscient God, ask you what your name is? He asks so that you know that coming into contact with Him, you will no longer be the same.

A question is designed to elicit information. Questions make us pause and dive deeper than we know we can go. Questions are what guide us toward what truly fulfils us. Through them we go deeper and we drop into the unknown. Through questions we ourselves unravel in contemplation. The more we grow our capacity by thinking, we begin to thirst after righteousness and search for knowledge as hidden treasure. The demoniac loudly asked, "What have I to do with You Jesus?" Because Jesus is a humbled servant, His ministry was not to kill, still, and destroy. Luke 4:18 gives a description of what Jesus came to earth to do when he said, "The Spirit of the Lord is upon me..." His ministry was to pluck up, to root up, to call out, and when the demoniac ran up to him, Jesus told legion to get out. Have you been delivered by something or someone that was holding you back? If so, consider giving God the praise.

What is your name? The reason why the man did not speak is because he was not the one in charge. We've all had those moments when we were disappointed because our order was messed up at a restaurant. Maybe the order was rushed. Maybe it was something the waiter said. Maybe the waiter forgot to put the fries in the bag that came with your combo. Maybe the waiter was having a bad day. At least this is what I told myself not long ago while celebrating my mom's birthday. Listen, it was my mother's birthday. Let's say on this day, I had enough of my order repeatedly having to be adjusted. On this day, for the cook, it was 3 strikes and you're out. I didn't want to speak to the server. I was upset, the waiter was upset, and I wanted to talk to the manager in charge. When Jesus showed up and asked the demoniac what his name was it was because He wanted to talk to the one who was in charge? While legion (2000) and Jesus were conversing, the possessed man was listening. The demoniac discovers that the reason why Jesus asked, "what is your name" is because when Jesus takes care of business, we are not the same. Greater is he that is in you than he that is in the world (1 John 4:14).

In (1 Peter 5:8), Peter declares, "Be sober, be vigilant because our adversary, the devil walketh about like a warring lion seeking whom he may devour." When lions attack, they don't always go after worthless prey, they go after the ones who are mighty, big, and tough; he attacks you now because you are a man or a woman of influence. Satan knew if that possessed man was set free, that his kingdom would be destroyed in that region of the Gadarenes. God has a plan and a purpose for you, your destiny. It's now the devil's will to block you and stop you. He has signed the warrant, he unleashes his forces against you because he knows that when the Lord gets through with you, you will not be the same.

Paul puts it this way in Romans 7:18, 19, "For I know that in me (that is, in my flesh,) dwelleth no good thing: for to will is present with me; but how to perform that which is good I find not. 19 For the good that I would I do not: but the evil which I would not, that I do." There is a war in my members, a division on the inside. Lord I need your help.

I love movies. I love good entertainment. One of my favorite movies is the "Titanic."

In 1996, treasure hunter Brock Lovett and his team aboard the research vessel *Akademik Mstislav Keldysh* search the wreck of *RMS Titanic* for a necklace with a rare diamond, the Heart of the Ocean. They recover a safe containing a drawing of a young woman wearing only the necklace dated April 14, 1912, the day the ship struck the iceberg. Rose Dawson Calvert, the woman in the drawing, is brought aboard *Keldysh* and tells Lovett of her experiences aboard *Titanic*.

In 1912 Southampton, 17-year-old first-class passenger Rose DeWitt Bukater, her fiancé Cal Hockley, and her mother Ruth board the luxurious *Titanic*. Ruth emphasizes that Rose's marriage will resolve their family's financial problems and retain their high-class persona. Distraught over the engagement, Rose considers suicide by jumping from the stern; Jack Dawson, a penniless artist, intervenes and discourages her. Discovered with Jack, Rose tells a concerned Cal that she was peering over the edge and Jack saved her from falling. When Cal becomes indifferent, she suggests to him that Jack deserves a reward. He invites Jack to dine with them in first class the following night. Jack and Rose develop a tentative friendship, despite Cal and Ruth being wary of him.

Following dinner, Rose secretly joins Jack at a party in third class. Jack and Rose had fallen in love. Cal the fiancé got mad and found himself chasing them with a gun throughout the ship. He was trying to pull Rose into his storm, but her peace was with Jack. With the ship sinking, and as her boat lowers, Rose decides that she cannot leave Jack and jumps back on board. Cal takes his bodyguard's pistol and chases Rose and Jack into the flooding first-class dining saloon. When the *Titanic* begins to sink, with people jumping and falling to their deaths, instead of Rose remaining on the life boat that was designed to save her and be delivered and set free, so she chooses instead to risk her life. She runs and gets off of it because she is so mesmerized for her Jack. I come to let somebody know today that Jack is not all that if you got to risk the welfare of your own life to get him! They both Jumped into the freezing water, and although Jack dies of hypothermia, with a blowing of a whistle I'm glad for her sake that life boat showed up. When I think about the story of Jesus, I find that He risked His own life just to save mine and yours and I get excited.

However, every achievement and every victory won is not connected to God. I have discovered that some battles are simply self-made war games, while other battles are birthed so that we can conclude that Jesus is the source of our strength, and that He is a Man of His Word. If the truth be told today, it is our weakness that makes way for God's strength. Someone else may suggest that the end date for who we think we are is the start date for what God purposed us to be. While this is true, when I am weak, what comes my way won't have its way. When I am weak, I am made strong. I want to suggest to you that in every facet of life we will face some kind of battle, and in the battle we win some and we lose some. However, Jesus has never lost a battle; He has never lost a case. What does that mean? If God is in it, even when it looks like defeat, the victory is already won. "What manner of man is this?" It's just Jesus the Son of the living God.

Everything that happens in your life that wears you down is just a building block destined to raise you up.

In Mark Ch. 4:35, on the same day, when the evening had come, He said to them "Let us cross over to the other side." When Jesus says let's go, He means what He says. When He calls He looks for us to respond. Going to the other side was not an option because there was someone in need on the other side of the river. When the Lord says, let's go, let's be willing to go. What compels you to go Jesus? "Somebody over there needs Me." It is a wonderful thing that Jesus is willing to rise against anything that stands in our way.

While on the journey Jesus rests for the preparation. He is tired. He sleeps through His storms so that He can get to our storms. Jesus took a nap because He was anxious to set you free. When He sets you free, go to work. For this reason, we have now come.

Jesus asks the question after silencing the storm, He says, "How is it that you have no faith?" The question today is, "How much more do you need to experience your right now for you to recognize what Jesus has done?" We often go without the assurance that we can make it and wonder if we could weather our storms. All we need to do is remember what He did last time.

In the gospel of Mark Ch. 5:1-2, Jesus and the disciples traveled to the other side of the sea, to the country of the Gadarenes. And when Jesus came out of the boat, immediately there met Him out of the tombs a man with an unclean spirit. He was a man who used to comb his hair in the morning, but now it's all matted, He used to dress nice, but now his Ralph Lauren outfit is soiled with dirt and blood. With desperation He runs to Jesus, but as he worships, he also defends what torments him. He wants to worship, but he doesn't want to be set free. He wants to be connected but doesn't want to be delivered because he is comfortable with his temporary relief. After Jesus commands the demon to come out, Jesus asks, "What is your name?" He began to speak in the singular, but because he asserted himself the voice declared, "My name is Legion." a Roman military term. How can a person be entrapped by that many demons? Well people have a problem identifying what demons are, some backbiters, some are cold hearted, some are proud, some are simply need to be connected to things that are not attached to God. The Bible states that they make a wish that they should go into the swine near them, Jesus permitted, and the pigs ran violently down a steep place in the sea and drowned. The swine herders were upset. Why? Because everybody is not going to rejoice with your deliverance because they are too focused on the pigs they lost.

I'm just glad that the boat showed up, when the rescue boat shows up, the throwing of life lines will come forth. When the boat shows up, there is fullness of joy. When the boat of God's presence shows up there are pleasures forever more. If Jesus is the Captain of my ship, I can weather any storm. If you need deliverance today, the boat will show up. If you feel all alone and in a place of darkness, the boat will show up. When you are in broken relationships the boat will show up. When there is sickness in the room, the boat will show up. When all hope is lost, God will show up!

The pig owner saw what happened, went into town and told it to everybody abroad. Now the Bible says in John 8:17 that the testimony of two witnesses is true. Devil you thought you were going about telling my business, but instead, you were just broadcasting the confirmation of my transformation.

Whenever God set us up for the blessing He will not only perform it, He will confirm it.

Reflections

1. We sell ourselves short sometimes trying to please everybody else. Have you ever seen progress by pleasing everyone else? If so, did you feel short changed? How important is it for others to recognize and acknowledge your value and what you bring to the table?

2. When you stand, there will be opposition. Can you think of an experience when you had to stand alone?

ROUND 4

BRUISED BUT NOT BROKEN!

And I saw in the right hand of Him who sat on the throne a scroll written inside and on the back, sealed with seven seals. Then I saw a strong angel proclaiming with a loud voice, "Who is worthy to open the scroll and to loose its seals?" And no one in heaven or on the earth or under the earth was able to open the scroll, or to look at it. So I wept much, because no one was found worthy to open and read the scroll, or to look at it. But one of the elders said to me, "Do not weep. Behold, the Lion of the tribe of Judah, the Root of David, has prevailed to open the scroll and to loose its seven seals."

Revelation 5:1-5 NKJV

Matlock is an American television legal drama, starring Andy Griffith. Matlock is known for recognizing hidden motives, identifying the perpetrators, and then confronting them in dramatic courtroom scenes. He could not put all of his faith in his associates because it would threaten his ability to solve every case. No matter how good Matlock was, he in fact did lose one case. No matter how good we think we are, the only one who has never lost a case is Jesus.

John the beloved disciple in his prime had been with Jesus. He himself was a recipient of the power that was distributed to the 12 other disciples. It was John who declared that in the beginning was the

Word and the Word was with God, and the Word was God. Without Him nothing made would have been made. The one who made it all, sees it all, and knows it all. All in all, John saw Jesus work miracles. He saw the lame walk. He saw the dumb talk. He saw the blind receive their sight. He saw lifeless men, and a little girl brought back to life. He put his trust in the Lord but that trust he put in Jesus, now after 60 years, has placed him in a dilemma.

John's got a problem. Here in the text is a 90-year-old man who has followed Jesus. By the lifting up of that name he has been blessed, but lifting up that name now has awarded him a hot seat, in a hot scorched pot of boiling oil. Nobody likes the hot seat, but if God is in it with you, you can know that nobody can be against you. When people come against you, and they find out that the Lord is with you, it makes them more upset. John is thrown onto the island of Patmos by Roman oppressors who have never accepted Jesus because they were of the darkness that could not comprehend the light from the beginning. Because the light shineth in darkness and the darkness comprehended it not, made them try and cut John's light out.

Come with me if you please on a trip down memory lane for a moment as we set the scene for our sermonic case. There is an evil one on the loose. And he is seeking to kill, steal, and destroy. He has been caught but has convinced a third of his folks that he is innocent. Some sided with him, and for that reason they now share in his fate. He has been caught, and the spiritual law enforcer reads him his Miranda Rights, "You have the right to remain silent. Anything you say can and will be used against you in a court of law. You have the right to an attorney. If you cannot afford an attorney, one will be provided for you. Do you understand the rights I have just read to you? With these rights in mind, do you wish to speak to me?" Revelation 5:1 the Bible says, "And I saw a book in the hand of him that sat on the throne, And I saw a strong angel proclaiming with a loud voice who is worthy to open the books and loose the seals there of?"

This Is How I Fight My Battles | 39

Plaintiff vs. Defendant in the court of Law.

The plaintiff in a court case is the person who has filed a complaint/charges against the defendant for prosecution by the courts, while the defendant is the person who is refuting the charges and is seeking to prove their innocence.

Imagine with me. Heaven is having a praise party, and John is in the midst of that praise, but the party is abruptly interrupted because here in the heavenly court session, here in the church, here in the text, somebody's elusive tradition makes them think that they have ascended above the stars of God and the heights of the clouds.

John is not weeping because of the ending of praise; John is weeping because he sees in view the reality that if the issue is not resolved will in fact shut out praise forever.

John's tears of Joy have now turned into sobbing sorrow. You can have joy one minute, and the next minute be filled with sorrow. Someone who has just won the publishing clearing house on one day is happy, but the next day saddened to find that they have terminal cancer.

What do you do when your joy has been crowded out by your tears? For the Bible declares that weeping may endure for a night, but joy comes in the morning and we accept that. What happens when your praise comes from an external comfort, rather than an inward reality that the trouble in your life won't last always?

I am convinced that when we follow Jesus, what He has prepared to illustrate, insinuate, and indicate to us cannot be determined by an external view, but if you are rolling with Him, expect to be displaced. What do you do when you've done all you can for the sake of Christ, and that good gets you in to trouble?

When the road is rough, and the going gets tough, when your way seems hopeless, always remember who you are and Whose you are. You may feel all alone, you may feel that no one cares, but the One who cares for you is worthy, and He is on your side.

There's one problem, we often praise God only when we're comfortable. We give God glory when He blesses us, but can you praise Him on your island of despair.

John the disciple is left to die on the isle of Patmos by those who hated him for preaching in Jesus' name. He has hope in his detriment because he sees with prophetic eyes that God has something in His possession that He is getting ready to release into the world according to Revelation 5:1. In order for something to be loosed it must first be unlocked. In Daniel 12:4, Daniel is told to close up the book and seal it up until the time of the end. For Knowledge shall increase. John is in the Spirit on the Lord's day. The angels are giving praise, glory, and honor to the One who sits on the throne, and while he and the angels are in praise, he sees a book. This book is not on the throne, it's not in the throne, it's not around the throne, it's not in your neighbor's car steaming, sweltering, and searing in the rearview window. It is in the hand of God.

The book is not gripped, it is not grasped, it is not clutched, it is not stuck, it is just resting in the right hand of Him who sits on the throne. John says when I saw the book, when I saw the scroll, immediately I saw a strong Angel declaring, decreeing, and challenging with a loud voice saying, "Who is worthy to open the book and loose the seals there of?" The Angel who is challenging and asking the question is a strong Angel, and he looks different than the rest of the cherubim, he looks different than the rest of the seraphim, he looks different than the rest of the four living creatures. This Strong Angel has a melody in his voice, this voice is like the sound of a roaring Lion who walketh about seeking who he may devour. This Strong Angel, intimidates, and he imitates, but John sees the real deal.

What God the righteous Judge is getting ready to release, or loose to us can only happen by an authoritative power that's greater than the forces of heaven and earth combined. No one was able to take the book, so John cried even more, but one of the elders saith unto him, weep not: behold, the Lion of the tribe of Judah, the Root of David, hath prevailed to open the book, and to loose the seven seals thereof. The reason why John was left all alone, is because God wanted John's blessing to be exclusive.

Have you ever appeared to court? Have you ever been in a mess? Have you ever been found guilty and you know you were guilty, but instead of justice received, God extended His mercy? You might be in a mess right now. You might be in a bad place right now. You might feel like giving up right now because you feel that you have been left on the island of set-backs, on the island of stress, on the island of sorrow, on the island of hardship, on the island of heartache, on the island of heartbreak. If so, always remember, where the Spirit of the Lord is, there is liberty.

And I beheld, and, lo, in the midst of the throne and of the four beasts, and in the midst of the elders, stood a Lamb as it had been slain, having seven horns and seven eyes, which are the seven Spirits of God sent forth into all the earth. The same one who had the power to prevail in the beginning is the same one who has the power to prevail right now.
Revelation 5:6 NIV

You are not alone.

Reflections

1. Although the disciple John found himself in an unfortunate situation while at Patmos, he learned that his current situation was not his final destination. John could not change his experience because God was trying to show him something through it. After reflection, can you identify at least one situation where you wanted to speed up the process, but instead glad you were patient enough to endure it?

2. John was on the Lord's side and it landed him in the hot seat. When we can't see what God is doing we tend to have the wrong perspective which makes us feel like were under attack. God allowed this Patmos experience so that John could know that there would be glory after this. Every advancement is preceded by some type of attack! Have you ever had to brace yourself because you knew the assignment or calling on your life was great? Did you see the attack making its way? What did you learn from your experience?

ROUND 5

THE ATTACK WAS SENT TO ELEVATE

Why do so many people run these days? Some of us run because it's good for our health. Some of us run because we expect a check in the mail. Some of us run because JC Penney's said everything is 60% off. What I'm trying to convey is that when we run it doesn't happen because our legs just start moving, something equivalent to a physical but mental switchboard in our head sends a neurologic shock to the nerves running from our heads to our legs.

- **Cerebrum** *(say: suh-REE-brum):* The cerebrum is the thinking part of the brain and it controls your voluntary muscles.
- **Cerebellum** *(say: sair-uh-BELL-um):* It controls balance, movement, and coordination (how your muscles work together).
- **Brain stem:** The brain stem is in charge of all the functions your body needs to stay alive, like breathing air, digesting food, and circulating blood
- **Pituitary** *(say: puh-TOO-uh-ter-ee)* **gland:** its job is to produce and release hormones into your body so you can grow.
- **Hypothalamus** *(say: hy-po-THAL-uh-mus):* The hypothalamus is like your brain's inner thermostat (that little box on the wall that controls the heat in your house) The average temperature should be 98.6°F or 37°C.

Elijah flees to Horeb

Something is happening here in the text, and it has caused our brother the Prophet, to not only sweat, it has caused him to lace up his spiritual Reeboks.

Now Ahab told Jezebel everything Elijah had done and how he had killed all the prophets with the sword. So Jezebel sent a messenger to Elijah to say, "May the gods deal with me, be it ever so severely, if by this time tomorrow I do not make your life like that of one of them." Elijah was afraid and ran for his life. When he came to Beersheba in Judah, he left his servant there, while he himself went a day's journey into the wilderness. He came to a broom bush, sat down under it and prayed that he might die. "I have had enough, Lord," he said. "Take my life; I am no better than my ancestors." Then he lay down under the bush and fell asleep. All at once an angel touched him and said, "Get up and eat."
There he went into a cave and spent the night. And the word of the Lord came to him: "What are you doing here, Elijah?"
1 Kings 19:1-9 NIV

Since we are made in God's image, God can regulate our minds and our nervous system at will. So, Elijah, what's your problem?

Elijah means the LORD is my God. Elijah is a prophet, who heard from God, who walked with God, who had excepted the provisions of God, who expected miracles from God, was given his Divine assignment from God. Elijah hated and confronted evil when it came to everybody else, but when it came to him, he started running, am I in the right church. Elijah was so bad and messed up that he ran from his troubles, but God thought he was so Good, that he would send him to the Mount of Transfiguration to lift up Jesus.

When did running from a problem ever become the prerequisite for answered prayer?

Unless the problem looks like a knife or a bullet let's face it, there are sometimes in life where you can't hang around and spectate or see what's about to happen next. Somebody starts yelling "Get your hand out my pocket." It's time to move, you got to get out of there. Jezebel was Queen, and she was used by the devil to send a message to buffet Elijah. Now the devil had devised this assault, this ambush, this attack, but it was under God's control. I'll pause right here to let somebody know troubles may rise, winds may blow, the threats by the evil assailant may be evident, but God's still in total control. I'm wondering if Ahab cared about his woman. If so he would've said, baby, don't you do that, the Bible says, he told her everything.

I live in a gated community, a controlled environment, I am kept by the Power of God. You ring the doorbell to get to me devil, if you get through it was with my Father's permission. Good or bad, if you get through, it was meant for my good. Listen, When the devil throws all he can at you at once, and what he throws begins to bear down on you, you ought to relieve yourself in the Lord. One song writer says it this way, "What a Friend We Have in Jesus." The song writer didn't say there is a friend, but what a Friend. The word "what" is used as an adverb to invite agreement, and it is given to delegate, designate, and to demonstrate what type of friend we have. Well what type of friend is He?

I'm so glad you asked, He is a friend... and because He is, I am more than a conqueror through Him who loves me (Romans 8:37). I am an overcomer by the blood of the Lamb and the word of my testimony (Revelation 12:11).

Your attitude can change your situation.

I'm thinking now, If God is all this, and much more to me, then the attack against me was sent improve me not to injure me. It was sent not to hurt me, but to help me. Elijah, the attack is just a gift and the gift was designed to elevate.

Instead of running from the attack, you will start praying for the attack. We're good with our defense, until the right button gets pushed.

When Ahab told Jezebel everything Elijah had done, she said, I got this, I'm going to push Elijah's buttons.

Elijah realizes that he cannot control the outcome, only God can. At Elijah's command, remember it was not going to rain until He said so. At Mt. Carmel he knew with confidence that he could trust God to show up, but now he cannot control a crazy queen named Jezebel who has failed to see what God did to the enemy the last time.

Your attitude can determine your altitude.

You were praying high at Mt. Carmel Elijah, but now that you are down in the valley you acting low. Elijah, it's time to push back. When you come back from your setback, remember that you don't have the right to remain silent. Let someone know that this is how you fight your battles.

This Is How I Fight My Battles | 47

God is still in control.

Reflections

1. Can you think of any attacks that kept you from moving forward?

2. Have you had an experience where the attack in your life pushed you toward fulfilling your goals or dreams?

ROUND 6
WHICH WAY SHOULD I RUN?

There is nothing like experiencing joy because of planning ahead. In fact, there are benefits for doing so. For instance, some people not only go to college, they finish. I can bear witness to this fact. Let me just say this, you can plan ahead, but if you don't make the necessary steps, if you procrastinate, if you settle for second place, if you are okay with being average, there will be missed opportunities, and a bunch of, "I wish I would have done this or that." Let me begin by saying, we have all seen them, we have all laughed at them, Cartoons. I was born in 1982, there were some good old cartoons on the set then: Thunder Cats, Looney Toons, you name it. Everybody likes action, everybody likes to see fast racing, and everybody wants to win. From a kid's perspective that's what you would see while watching the cartoons like "Wacky Races" an American animated comedy series written by Larz Bourne, Dalton Sandifer, Tom Dagenals, and Michael Maltese. The plot is that the villain drives a purple rocket-powered car with an abundance of concealed weapons and the ability to fly. Dick Dastardly was the terrible mustache-twirling villain; Muttley is his wheezily snickering dog henchman.

Dastardly's race strategy revolves around using his machines great speed to get ahead. He had all the tools to be first, but instead of just being first, and pressing forward he would get ahead of the racers, and then set a trap to stop them to maintain the lead. Unfortunately, for him his plan would backfire causing him to fall back into last place every time. How can we make since of this? If you are honest with yourself, you can conclude with me that there is still a bunch of wacky races going on in our society today. From the White House, to the Church pulpit, there are those who are so in it for themselves that they forget the purpose of why they are in the race. The race is designed for people or things to move swiftly. Ultimately, it is designed for them to finish their race. When I race, I just want to finish.

Have you been in a race lately? Long time ago right? Some people are setup to win. The playing field is the same, but often what place you come in sometimes is beyond your control. In the society in which we live I often find it difficult to win sometimes, because of the odds that are stacked against me just because of the color of my skin. What's happening? If that's your question, we are missing the things that are said and are being done with people of color. Discrimination is everywhere, but since I live in America, I shout from the hill tops, "Wake Up America!" Perhaps America has never slept and has known always what its intentions were under the guidance of certain vicarious powers, and a "shadow government" ran by codes. Could it be that the reason why we see injustice today, even after the battle at Antietam in 1862, that in January 1, 1863 the Emancipation Proclamation signed sealed and delivered by Abraham Lincoln is still inadequate to make slaves forever free. I know that the Emancipation of Proclamation was a document, but not any kind of document, a document signed with promise by a president. What happened to the promise? What was discussed at the table when Americas founding documents such as the U.S. Constitution and Bill of Rights were constructed? Was it formulated for my good, your good? Where do you fit in with "We The People?"

These are questions that haunt me when I see, even in 2020, young African American men and women being gunned down after being racially profiled, something 'ain't' right folks. Oh yeah, we hang our hats on this patriotic statement, "All men are created equal and are endowed by their Creator." However, the assimilation has never ended, and it has been assumed that the dominant will always prevail. Remember now in the Wacky Race the character who is dishonest can turn the sign to make the other cartoon characters (people) who are racing go in the wrong direction, but the ones who go in the wrong direction somehow still win the race, and no matter what it looks like the villain never succeeds.

In this life there will be some plots against your moving forward, your pressing your way, your success, your win, your victory. In our current society, your kneeling down for injustice, your standing up for what is right, all that come against you will not prosper. Revolution has always come out of a fight. It is time to fight. How? With our minds. It is time for civil disobedience once more. The same kind that ended the Fugitive Slave Act, Jim Crow laws, segregation. What does that look like? In the 60's, marches, sit-ins, bus boycotts, but now just simply taking a knee during the proclaiming of the National Anthem gets national attention.

The answer to systemic racism in this nation, is the acknowledgment that it does exist. It exists everywhere, from the school house to the church house. What our society currently needs is an innovative approach to secure equality within the diverse community it caters to. Social change is what's needed on this playing field to ensure that all will have their share of both learning and contributing to the work shared. For the most part we are to be the change that we want to see in others. After several years of strategizing, listening, and advocating for change, we can follow through with a vision, and with a mission to accomplish the work in helping locally and globally.

Revolution always come out of a fight.

Reflections

1. The playing field is the same for everyone but sometimes the place you come in is beyond your control. What do you do when all odds are stacked against you? Your will to continue is powered by your purpose. After all, any endeavor driven is fueled by your purpose. What motivates you to give it all you got?

2. List three things that have challenged you. Can you list anything that you benefited from experiencing these challenges?

ROUND 7
THE NATURE OF OPPRESSION

One thing that I have come to realize is that nobody is able to connect with everybody all the time. If the truth be told, some people are shy, some are not social, or even approachable. In every aspect of life whether it's in your relationship or your profession, you cannot get close to people that you don't touch, people who you don't impact. Although this is true, what do you do when people are determined to be distant? I am convinced that the answer is embedded sometimes in who people are, or what they have actually done. In Joshua's day, Achan had done something which brought oppression to his house. Is this not the norm these days? Homes are broken up because someone took something and replaced it with something else. For example, when joy is replaced with jealousy, when laughter is replaced with nagging, when saying 'I'm sorry' is replaced with pointing the finger at someone else, oppression comes knocking and oppression knows how to compete well.

Ai Destroyed

Then the Lord said to Joshua, "Do not be afraid; do not be discouraged. Take the whole army with you and go up and attack Ai. For I have delivered into your hands the king of Ai, his people, his city and his land. You shall do to Ai and its king as you did to Jericho and its king, except that you may carry off their plunder and livestock for yourselves. Set an ambush behind the city."

Then the Lord said to Joshua, "Hold out toward Ai the javelin that is in your hand, for into your hand I will deliver the city." So Joshua held out toward the city the javelin that was in his hand. As soon as he did this, the men in the ambush rose quickly from their position and rushed forward. They entered the city and captured it and quickly set it on fire.
Joshua Chapter 8:1-2, 18-19 NIV

When I look back over my life I begin to discover that God is a God of preparation. You only prepare for what you expect. When you look back over your life you begin to reflect on the people who made a difference in your life. And part of the reason why I've had success in life is because of what others have poured into me. Every success is ordered by God. I'm reminded of loved ones who poured into me. I reminded of my grandmother Mable who would listen to me silently and say "Yeah" about the things I had to say about God, I'm reminded of the jokes and stories from my Grand-father. He shared with others that I would do great and be great someday because of my desire to know more and want more.

I'm reminded of my Aunt Regina who called me Pastor before I became Pastor. She shared her last words with me before she died as we sang songs together. Songs like, *There is Power in the Name of Jesus* and *Break Every Chain*. What was she trying to show me while we sang together? The music therapist said, "Do you have another request?" And because she had trouble speaking, she said "Battlefield." I could not make out what she was trying to say until she shouted out again, "Battlefield." It was then that I recognized the song she was requesting, "I Am on the Battlefield for My Lord." Through the song selection she was suggesting to me that even when you are discouraged in life, keep fighting. When folks give up on you, don't give up on God, keep fighting. Listen, you are not in the battle by yourself. You don't have to fight in your own strength. God is going to get some glory out of what you go through, just keep fighting. Fighting is what leaders do. Leading is what leaders do, an although we have elected officials and leaders in church, in community, in our nation, all of you are a leader too. Today, the only way to preserve life is to fight. The day you stop fighting is the day you start dying. Dying is what happens when we begin to lose our grip in life. When we cease to thrive, we cease to continue. You can tell how real something is by how much it continues and if you can walk away from something so easily then maybe you were never attached to it. In this season, break away from everything thing that suggests to you that you can just sit back and wait for your blessings, for miracles. Go to war for what you want. Press your way into the presence of God. Watch Him perform His work.

Continuing will cost you something. When we have an encounter with the eternal it will position us for greatness. Let's face it. There are many of us that are so acquainted with having church, without a worship experience. Like a car wash, we come in, sit down, get wet, splashed with the dew of God's word, but never get clean. Sometimes we are guilty of wanting microwavable experiences where we thought we could just enjoy the moment without being touched, having to deal with our actions that got us dirty before our wash. What good would it be to come into this place, overdose on church, on community service, but never experience the glory of God. What if we all showed up today, but love decided to take the day off? When love leaves the building, we become agents of the institution but no change agents in the community. It is certain that what the world needs, what the community needs, what the church needs is a safe place, a welcoming place and love is the answer. Like a woman who has been put on bed rest to preserve her child, we need a safe place. A safe place to deliver what God is about to birth through us so that we can impact the world. In Bible prophecy the woman is the church, and the community within now reaches out to them and they are in need of a safe place. A welcoming place to deliver blessings.

We have a responsibility to relieve those who are oppressed, but that is hard to do when you are depressed. The member shall remain nameless, but had the nerve to tell me, "I can't work with a certain people." Here is the scripture used for their argument, "By their fruit ye shall know them."

Although the text is relevant, just because you know people's fruit don't mean you are rooted. Clearly, this person was "cutting up," rooted maybe, but definitely not grounded. (Matthew 7:16-17) Guess what? I notice by personal testimony, those who are not grounded will not grow. Let's face it, many people walk away from the church building, and when they do, people suggest that they left God. This is far from the truth. However, people walk away from departmental leadership and community service altogether, and most of the time it is because they were not planted right. No matter what line of work you're in there must be some form of training. If you get planted right, you will grow right. Sometimes we plant in bad soil, we root people in ministries we know they can't grow in. If that don't kill them, the wrong climate will. Bad attitudes suffocate Community. The reason why we often face defeat is because when we are commanded to move forward everybody is not with us. And where there is no plan, no plot, no effort, no vision, no tool or spiritual javelin to fight, the people perish.

Joshua 7:11-13, in this prophetic passage, the person of the Holy Spirit, is showing us that there is tension in this text and in the life of this particular community. In this community, many are concerned that the purpose for the community has not been affirmed by God who claims through His covenant that HE will be with them. So God has a conversation with Joshua, and says, "Don't sweat it." Let's face it, we go through what we go through because we fail to remember what God did the last time. Take your shoes off your feet.

The very reason we often lose our authenticity, is because we lose our identity. It's like claiming to be a Christian, but at the same time hating people. It's like holding a position in church but never doing anything with it. It's like being on a spiritual treadmill where you are gaining miles, but not going anywhere. A lot of motion, but no progress. A lot of noise but no music, and when there is no progress, no process, no profession people will lay on their couch of sorrow and cover up with the blanket of insecurity and anxiety. This causes them to have stagnant, stale, and stank attitudes that lead to discouragement. Discouragement in this Hebrew text means to be internally broken or internally cut down, which causes one to collapse. If the truth be told, we want to be transformed but we don't want to be stretched. When God told Joshua not to be discouraged, he was suggesting that it was time to stay woke, and it's hard to stay woke when your community is a mess, internally broken. You are tired, you are ready to do something no longer through discouragement, but now by encouragement from God. God is saying to us, "Wake up." The nature to oppression is avoidable, hold to what you have and make it work.

God meant it for my good.

Problem is defined as, a matter or a situation regarded as unwelcome or harmful and needed to be dealt with and overcome. One thing that I am sure of is that the world is full of problems. The world in and of itself has no ability to create unwelcomed circumstances, but people do. You can be having a great day, then problems will show up on you and say, "Here I am." When problems show up I've learned that you can do two things, become part of it, or fix it. It is hard to fix what you can't see. The Bible declares in Ephesians 6:12 that, "We wrestle not against flesh and blood but against principalities, against powers, against rulers of the darkness of this world, against spiritual wickedness in high places." From the heavens to the earth, from the White House to the Poor House, we have seen problems. When problems show up, there is a willpower that God has put inside of us to handle it when it arises. Sometimes the handling it, and fixing it, only come by way of our faith. The truth is, everyone has problems and it doesn't matter what line of work you're in, how much money you have, what ethnicity or gender you are, married, single, beautiful, or avoiding the mirror, we got problems.

God allows your problems to show up, but your problems serve a purpose. But know right now, everything will work out for your good.

Philippians 1:12-13 states, "But I want you to know, brethren, that the things which happened to me have actually turned out for the furtherance of the gospel, so that it has become evident to the whole palace guard, and to all the rest, that my chains are in Christ."

Paul takes us right into the chamber room of his text. He is an accomplished man, he is an educated man, a devout Pharisee, who recognized that he must be all things to all people. He was respected in one click but rejected by another click. He was hated by many and loved by a few. Paul is a great man who God has raised up to proclaim, decree, and declare the word of God, but now he is incarcerated, now he is held captive, his company now is a Roman Solider, a ball, and some chains. Paul has been arrested because of his background, he has been religiously, and spiritually profiled, and it has landed him in a dungeon. But the dungeon was set up by God to have a resting place to pen the word we have today. Paul had a problem, but his problem served a purpose. Anybody ever been somewhere they didn't want to be in a circumstance that you wanted to get out of, but you couldn't because you were too emotionally captive to what was happening? Nobody knows his pain, nobody he loves sees his tears, even those who he is writing to can never fully understand the weight of his calling as he is now in shackles. This was Paul's reality. What do you do when you have spent most of your life helping everybody else around you, now you're stuck all by yourself? If this is you, don't be alarmed, don't be upset, have no fear because it's here in your mess, in your captivity, in your stress that God is going to work things out for your good.

Whatever happens to me now, will happen because of what God is getting ready to do. Paul had preached the Gospel, he had taught in the synagogues, he has seen the moving of God's Spirit, but he has been blinded, he has recovered his sight, he has been whipped on three occasions, he's had a bounty over his head the haters said, "We won't eat or sleep until Paul is dead." Paul had been stoned and drug outside the city, left for dead. Paul had been shipwrecked three times, he has been bitten by a snake, physically and spiritually, he has been bitten, but he is not broken because he recognizes that his problems are actually opportunities for God to do something new.

If God is going to be great in your life, you got to let Him be great when things are going your way, and when things are not. You're saying how can things be going well with me, and at the same time there is a lot of hell in me? How can I be set free, and at the same time broken because of what I'm going through? Paul is trying to suggest to us that what we are going through is not all that bad. Sometimes we may have to go through some troublesome difficulties in life, so God can remind us of what He is getting ready to do for us, Help is on the way. Paul declares in Romans 8:18, "For I reckon that the sufferings in this present moment are not worthy to be compared to the glory that shall be revealed in us."

Remember Paul was messed up, his name was Saul, he did what he wanted when he wanted, had folks dragged to court, killed, and watched Stephen get stoned. When God makes a wonderful change in your life no matter what you are facing, you will thank God that He did not leave you where you were. I thank you God for my captivity because in it I now see my destiny.

Paul is so in tune with God, he begins to write while in chains and he says, what the devil has meant for my bad, God has turned it around for my good. Troubles may rise, times may get tough, but God will keep you in perfect peace whose mind is stayed on him.

It is evident that the reason why I am who I am, and what I am is because of Christ. I may be in chains, but my chains are just Gods way of locking me in with him. GOD MEANT IT FOR MY GOOD.

Everything that happens in your life that wears you down is just a building block destined to raise you up.

It's for your good.

Reflections

1. Part of the reason why I've had success in life is because of what others have poured into me. Can you think of three people who poured into you personally? List them. After listing them, reach out to them and thank them, or someone close to them.

2. What are you willing to do to make your church or community a more welcoming space for others?

ROUND 8

IGNORE THE INVISIBLE, TRUST THE IMPOSSIBLE

Invincible – The plot, the scheme

Though persecution has been an undesirable fixture of the church since the time of Christ, the evil reign of Emperor Nero Augustus Caesar in Rome was destined to make matters even worse. Peter the apostle has been in dangerous positions before, but there was something different about this experience from the rest of his experiences. This letter found in 1 Peter Ch. 1, is the Apostles' attempt to prepare, comfort, and urge the believers in Asia Minor to remain strong despite their suffering.

Let's face it, sometimes it difficult to be strong or remain strong once we have been hurt. We do not necessarily like challenges when they come, but because we are more than conquerors we rise to the occasion. Have you ever suffered from fear, anxiety, suffered with not knowing where your next meal would come from, not knowing if you would have money left to pay all the bills, not knowing what your next move was going to be on your career path? Then you can sympathize with the Apostle's experience.

Imagine Peter with a sense of knowing that tomorrow he would be put to death? Had you been there during the time of this fiery trial in A.D. 62, if you had to take a front row seat to see and hear the Apostle's speech, it probably would have gone this way, "We are at the end of our rope but I understand that it is by the mercy of God that we are not consumed. If the devil had his way, we would've been wiped out a long time ago, but when the enemy comes in like a rushing flood, the Lord lifts a standard against him." Here's the problem, many of us just simply do not know how to make distress calls. Distress calls communicate to search parties that you urgently need lifesaving intervention. In times of certain storms, you might have to dial 911, but what happens when your 911 needs a 911. When you are in distress you got to know how to call on the name of Jesus. There are times in this life when you just can't find your way, but understand and know that God will show up and make a way. For the Lord has said, "I have spoken these things that in me you might have peace, in this life you shall have tribulation but be of good cheer for I have overcome the world." John 16:33. God wants you to know that in your distress, in your storm, in your time of trouble, even through your opposition, even while against all odds, God is able to do exceedingly abundantly above all you could ever ask or think.

Instead of running to your friends all the time when trouble comes your way, why don't you taste and see for yourself that the Lord is good, and that His mercy endureth forever. I am convinced, that after searching for eternity you will discover that there is no one like Jesus. When He speaks, why don't you consider it done. When I look into the mirror I see how He was able to take nothing and make something out of it, Jesus, the image of the invisible God, Jesus, the one in which the fullness of the God head dwells, Jesus, learn to call on His name.

God is able to do exceedingly above all I could ever ask or think.
Ephesians 3:20 KJV

Peter remembers that the devil desired to have him, and to sift him as wheat. (Luke 22:31) Now he is at the point in his life where he is ready to be crucified upside down. Upside down was Peter's preference, but God is not calling you to come and be crucified upside down, God is calling you to live your life, Holy and acceptable, right side up. He's calling you now to be vessels turned up right to receive the Spirit of the Living God. Such as it was with Peter, it should be now with us.

It is evident that the reason we go through what we go through, is so that we can go through. Too many of us have been pacified for so long, that when troubles come our way, we have tendencies to revert to our old ways. Too often on our spiritual journey we want every chain broken, but I am convinced, here me now, I am convinced that some of the trials, and some tribulations that we go through are not so much that we should call on the Lords name, but rather praise His holy name. Our worship is what informs our time spent with God, and the reason why some of us can't praise Him right now, can't praise in our trial, won't praise Him during our test, can't praise Him even in the good times is because we sometimes do not spend quality time with Him.

However, your struggle or your storm whether you know it or not was set up by God to demonstrate His abundant mercy, and the lively hope of His name. I'm glad to let you know today that we serve a God who doesn't mind standing up, even during storms. He will declare, "Peace be still." (Mark 4) For the Bible says that, "He has begotten us again by His abundant mercy and the lively hope of the resurrection of Jesus Christ from the dead." (1 Peter 1:5) In other words Peter is saying, Some of you have been scattered, you have displaced through the lense of yesterday's slavery, but now policies to oppress immigration, recent catastrophic events, devastations from Hurricane Harvey and Hurricane Irma, earthquakes in Mexico, fires in California. Some of you don't know what your next move will be, some of you are in despair, but through it all my friend, in the midst of what you are going through, God has a plan, and the end thereof will be greater than the past. By faith go ahead and begin rejoicing right now for what the Lord has already done even if you don't see it. Your sanity is on the line here.

> **Accept the reality of you not understanding what God is doing, but rather rejoice because you know that He is the one leading the way.**

This is what I call ignoring the invincible, but embracing the Impossible. Accepting the reality of you just simply not understanding what God is doing, but rather rejoice because you know that He is the One leading the way. For the Bible declares, "Before I called, He has already answered." (Isaiah 65:24, KJV) Therefore, If you are going to make it through, you've got to get to the point where you can persevere, you got to get to the point where you can speak a word over your own life, you got to get to the point, where you can speak to your situation and say like Job, "Though He slay me, yet will I trust in Him." You've got to get to the point where you just simply understand that weeping may endure for a night, but joy comes in the morning. Paul said it this way, "We are troubled on every side, yet not distressed, we are perplexed, but not in despair, we are persecuted, but not forsaken, we are cast down, but not destroyed." What's coming ladies and gentlemen is better than what's been. In the process, you got to learn how to ignore the invisible, and rejoice in the Impossible.

That passage of scripture was written so that the audience would know that real Christian experience would be one where people recognize that they are able to persevere despite whatever they were going through. That which Christ is trying to reveal in us, even now has not only been reserved in heaven, you can experience the glory right now. For the Bible declares in 1 Peter 1:5, "We are kept by the Power of God." When I read that one sentence, I did not have to read any further, I did not have to go into any commentary. I didn't have to know Greek terminology, but I chose too, and now with my homiletical license, and standing here with more than just an assumption, with blessed assurance I believe that you can agree with me also that we are kept by the Power of God's word.

If we look at the word "power," in the English dictionary you would discover that this term is used in several ways, but what stands out the most is when it is defined as a "legal authority." It was a legal transaction that had taken place when the blood of Jesus was shed. We are reconciled with God. If that's not good enough, the term "Power" in the Greek, in this particular text is "dynamis," which means force, either literal or figurative. The term power in this text is for specifically miraculous power. In other words, Peter is saying, that it is a miracle in and of itself that you are kept by the power of God. The term power has ability, abundance, meaning, might, works mightily, it is a mighty deed, it has strength, it can be violent, it is a wonderful work.

Instead of focusing on what you can't do, start focusing on what you can do.

God wants you to know that in your distress, in your storm, in your time of trouble, even through your opposition, against all odds, God is able to do exceedingly abundantly above all you could ever ask or think.

Reflections

1. The power in which we are kept is through faith and God's abundant mercy.

2. Let the genuineness of your faith be found unto praise.

3. Even though you can't see the hand of God, you believe, and because you believe, you can rejoice with joy unspeakable and full of Glory.

ROUND 9
EMBRACE THE IMPOSSIBLE

Dreams do come to life, but what good is a dream that is never pursued. We all have dreams, and if you can remember them the next morning, they are so interesting that we want to have them explained to us. I remember several dreams that I've had, but there is one that stands taller than them all. At the time, I was out of high school just working and still living with my parents. As I was resting on the couch in the den, I had a dream. In the dream, I was in a basketball gym all alone. I noticed that I had on a black clergy robe with red crosses on it. I walked directly to the free-throw line with a ball in hand. I stood, and suddenly, I took off soaring without a running start.

Maybe 20 feet above the rim coming down with a lean in dunk. Now this was an unusual dream, but what is so fascinating about this dream is that I dreamed it more than once. Same gym, same pastoral robe, same lean-in dunk, but with nobody present to cheer, and nobody present to bear witness of what had just been done. If any of you are into basketball, then you know that any dunk that is attempted from the distance of the free-throw line, is awesome. It was Michael Jordan versus Dominique Wilkins in 1989 where Jordan came in from the baseline with a lean in monster jam. I want to suggest to you that the dunk in my dream was ten times better. As a young man, I began to seek God, I began to establish a relationship with Jesus, and would you know, my relationship with Him made all the difference in my life.

Through the dream, God was showing me my destiny, but it was up to me to have it fulfilled.

In 2007, I was working for a construction company alongside my uncle. It was there in Vicksburg, Mississippi at a restaurant when I mentioned that I was going to pursue the ministry to accept God's invitation. After sharing, my uncle's advice to me went this way, "Make sure you have all your ducks in a row." At that moment, I didn't know exactly what angle he was coming from, but I truly believe that he was telling me to get my house in order. One thing that I was sure of in that moment was that I could not measure up to what people thought I should, or could be. Not because of the inability to perform, but simply because of people not being able to see the fire that ignited my soul. With a made up mind, if you ever say yes to God, He will position you and confirm that you can accomplish the task He gives. What I have discovered after all of those years, that when God has given you a vision, a dream, He expects you to step into it. Not only mentally, but physically also. Let your next move be your best move.

Through the dream God was showing me my destiny, but it was up to me to have it fulfilled.

Let's look at King Hezekiah, 2 Kings 20. Hezekiah was sick unto death, but God spared his life. When the opportunity came for him to be a witness, and show how great his God was, he showed his possessions instead. Hezekiah showed the envoys from Babylon what he had, he never showed them his God. After reading the story sometimes we don't like what God is doing, sometimes things just don't make sense (the sickness), but God's thoughts are higher and so are His ways. At the end of it all, you will discover that even when bad things occur in life, they were still meant for your good. Good deeds do not position us for greatness, but let me tell you, serving God does. It's not about who we are, our positions, our titles, our last name, our connections, what matters most is whose we are. Here is the reality, what we feel is usually the drive for what we do, and the decisions we make. If you have lost the battle in your mind, then you are already defeated on your way toward the action you are going to take. Some of us want to be transformed but we don't want to be stretched. If I'm stretched, I might not feel right, I might not look the same.

However, we need a change of heart, and a right Spirit renewed in us. Did you know that most of us, if not all of us at some point in time are unprepared to deal with the lifestyle changes that God has purposed for our lives? If ever you choose to bring change, be positive, be intentional, God will cause you to have an encounter with Him. If the truth be told, we don't like every encounter with God because sometimes the experience causes us to take a step back. Especially after the setback, it's at this place where you will discover that no matter where you go, what you do, what you finish, it's never over until God say it over. When God blesses and gives life, it is because He wants to bring people in our lives that are in need of our testimony.

When you are determined to do all in your power to save rather than destroy, God will give provision for opportunity. Opportunities will cause faith wheels to move, and no matter what it looks like, you will come to know that it's not over until God says it's over.

- **Principle #1:** God will position you for greatness through your test.
- **Principle #2:** Recognize where you are in the Lord. His will is to show you that it's time to stretch toward your position.

Back to embracing the impossible. I attempted to "get the ducks in a row", save money, pay off bills, get my wife to believe in the dream, everything I could do to move forward. Would you know that I quickly discovered that no matter how hard I tried to get things in order, there was this inner belief that the task at hand, was nearly impossible for me. Here's your chance to shout. I'm writing to let you know right now that the impossible was just God's chance to work a miracle in my life. Many nights I prayed at the foot of the bed that my wife and kids were in. Many nights I would read just to build my confidence that the plan God had chosen for me would be self-embraced, not by others, but by me. I told God if this is going to happen, He had to set it up, He must make the provision, and that He must give me the proof that He was calling me to serve in ministry. Be careful what you ask for folks, its coming.

So, three years later I turned in my application to admissions at Oakwood University in Huntsville Alabama. It was almost time for class to begin when I received my acceptance letter. That was the beginning of something great, but then while matriculating through school, I had a tough time because my family was not with me, my relationship with Tabatha was strained just by being absent from home, especially because Caleb had just been born in 2009. I remember going into the counselor's office to ask what I must do to withdraw from school. The counselor told me she was getting ready to go to lunch, come back at one o'clock. When I got to her office she began to ask what the problem was, and I began to share. I didn't think she had the time to listen to my pitiful situation. To make a long story short, when I was done explaining she stated, "Who told you that this was going to be an easy task? The choices that we make today can affect us for a lifetime." If I had not listened to her I wouldn't have graduated with my Bachelors in 2012, or my Masters in Pastoral Studies in 2015, now working on my Doctorate. From the mountain top, God is declaring to us, that our problems are not necessary problems, they are rather God's opportunities to show us who He is and what He is about to do next in our life.

I said all of this just to let you know that you need to embrace the impossible. When the things that you want to pursue in life appear to be beyond your reach, do what you can. Set some goals, get your priorities straight, "Get your ducks in a row," but most importantly trust God. Trust the dream, trust the vision as He makes provision for you to tap, or plug in to your destiny.

God is declaring to us, that our problems are not necessarily problems, they are rather God's opportunities to show us who He is, and what He is about to do next in our life. Embrace the impossible.

Reflections

1. Have you ever been impressed that God was leading you or showing you what He wanted you to do in a dream or vision? Did you go after it? If yes, write it down. If no, when will you begin?

2. God has used storms, fiery furnaces, lion's dens, prisons, things that we do not desire just to have an encounter with Him. Has there been an experience you endured that you didn't request for, but you know it came to you to draw you closer to God?

ROUND 10
IT'S YOUR TIME

Hezekiah's reign had begun with such great promise. He had initiated efforts designed to effect purity within the practice of religion and integrity within the political process. He removed the high places, broke the images, cut down the groves, and broke into pieces the brazen serpent which had become the occasion for idolatry in Judah. But alas, after fourteen years of growing, a foe which had lurked menacingly on the horizon for all that time reared itself full length and dared to challenge all that Judah had been about. (2 Kings 18:29-33)

IT – When some of us get mad, instead of saying he said or she said, we say "It said." The word It can be a connotation where the light has come on in the mind. When the mama said to her child you going to get it, then we can conclude that the "IT" she is referring to, will show up in the shape, form, and fashion of a good old whipping. The word It, is a possessive word. Whatever the it was, it caused Hezekiah to go into the House of the Lord. What somebody in this room is standing in need of right now, I'm convinced that It can be found in the house of the Lord.

> And it came to pass, when king Hezekiah heard it, that he rent his clothes, and covered himself with sackcloth, and went into the house of the LORD. And he sent Eliakim, which was over the household, and Shebna the scribe, and the elders of the priests, covered with sackcloth, to Isaiah the prophet the son of Amoz. And they said unto him, Thus saith Hezekiah, This day is a day of trouble, and of rebuke, and blasphemy: for the children are come to the birth, and there is not strength to bring forth. It may be the LORD thy God will hear all the words of Rabshakeh, whom the king of Assyria his master hath sent to reproach the living God; and will reprove the words which the LORD thy God hath heard: wherefore lift up thy prayer for the remnant that are left.
>
> *2 Kings 19:1-4*

Isn't it funny how we go running to God only when we find ourselves in trouble?

The Bible says that Hezekiah heard IT. What's the IT? The IT is the stuff that kept them from moving into their destiny, the IT was the stuff that, polluted their minds into believing for that there was no hope, the IT was the stuff that was not allowing them to PUSH.

But Hezekiah the Bible says, went into the house of the Lord?

I don't know why you came, or what you stand in need of right now, but I am convinced that whatever it is, It's in the House of the Lord. Can I hear you say "Church?"

I want you to think about the critical moments of pregnancy. The process of giving birth is incredibly tiring, stressful, and to be frank it can be very dangerous. At the end of it all is often a joyous experience. Most mothers would say they felt like they didn't have the strength to see it through, but they still pushed.

Isaiah 36:1, "Now it came about in the fourteenth year of King Hezekiah, Sennacherib king of Assyria came up against all the fortified cities of Judah and seized them."

One by one the cities of Israel fell into his hand, finally he gets to Jerusalem, and instead of attacking he offers them the idea of surrendering. His speech was very intimidating as you will see. Before we get there I want to talk about one of the types of strength that Hezekiah realized he no longer had.

The text we read is part of a communication from Hezekiah King of Israel when the King of Assyria entered Israel and began attacking and overtaking many cities. He sent word to Isaiah and said, tell God what's going on here, and specifically tell him that we are in danger of losing this child (our destiny, our nation, the promise of this land). We are at a critical moment, I sense it could be the time for the birth of something wonderful, but we are completely out of strength to deliver the baby.

When you come to the place where God is trying to have you experience new life, you come to birth, but can't experience the birth because of the lack of power to give the final push, that final press and prod.

Isaiah 66:9 (ESV) says, "Shall I bring to the point of birth and not cause to bring forth?" says the Lord: "shall I, who cause to bring forth, shut the womb?" says your God.

Hezekiah felt abandoned, he felt alone, he felt like he was the only one left carrying the shield of faith, and he sends word to Isaiah, "I don't know if I can keep this up."

In Genesis 32:24 we read, "And Jacob was left alone; and there wrestled an angel with him until the breaking of the day."

He was alone, he was in a fight, until the breaking of the day. You need to do what you have to get your blessing, even if it is uncomfortable, difficult, hard, it's your blessing.

Delivery is expected, normal, and next – but not without strength. Power is needed to birth time's fullness. Like a mother's need of strength to affect that final "push" through the birth canal. Such a push is delicate and dangerous at the same time. Power is needed because in birth there is pain in process of passage. Jesus saw past the pain. Not even the Son of God could escape this. Redemption's new life was not possible except by Calvary's pain. The sinner's new life is not possible except he knows the pain of confessed guilt. We often forget the pain factor in trying to usher in history's possibilities and are unprepared to experience the agonies of its birth process.

The enemy to our aspirations sometimes seem stronger than the sources of our inspiration. When you find yourself in trouble you ought to just bless the Lord anyhow.

> And Hezekiah received the letter of the hand of the messengers, and read it: and Hezekiah went up into the house of the LORD, and spread it before the LORD. And Hezekiah prayed before the LORD, and said, O LORD God of Israel, which dwellest between the cherubims, thou art the God, even thou alone, of all the kingdoms of the earth; thou hast made heaven and earth.'
> 2 Kings 19:14-15 KJV

God could easily say to us Proverbs 1:23-27, "Because I called and you refused, you didn't hear me, I will laugh at your calamity." But His grace steps in and He provides.

No matter how many times the Assyrian army had conquered other nations, they were not going to reroute or change the plans of God. Side note: If Joseph was here he would tell you that even the jealousy of my brothers could not change God's plan. In fact, Joseph needed to get to Egypt. He could not have made it on time, nor so quickly, had he not been sold into slavery.

What is interesting is that when the Assyrians come to Jerusalem instead of attacking with military might they attack instead with words. As a child, I often heard it growing up, "Sticks and stones may break my bones, but words will never hurt me." If that was not the biggest lie ever told. You got talked about, and it took everything in you to keep from coming unglued, unlatched, and unchristen, aka lost your religion. In this life, sometimes it's not about what you do but rather what you say. What good is charity if done with good intentions, but then utilized the wrong way. For some, all they need to here is a little intimidation and they will run for the hills. Let me be very clear about this, if you are going to live for God and stand on his word, you are going to have to face and learn to deal with intimidating words spoken by the enemy.

Life and death is in the power of the tongue. For instance, if a mother continues to tell her child that he or she will never be nothing, it may just come true. For the children, after hearing these things are robbed of the possibility that they can be somebody. I came to serve the devil notice today; I am not who you say I am. What I am to become is ready now to spring forth, so get out of my way. If nothing happens it's not because God is not able, it may just be because you are scared to push and press your way - for the children have come to birth.

Bringing to birth God's promises is often akin to warfare. It is a fight often with armies with superior forces. The Bible says, "We are not fighting against flesh and blood! There are powers of darkness, spiritual wickedness in high places." (Ephesians 6:12 KJV) Whenever you are troubled by the thought of who you are fighting against, calm yourself by reminding yourself of who it is on your side in the fight with you. Greater is He that is in you than he that is in the world.

What you are to become is ready now to spring forth. Tell the enemy to get out of your way. If nothing happens it's not because God is not able. In the past you may have been afraid to push and press your way. It's time to push!

Stay Connected.
Stay Plugged to the Source.
-Brian Thomas

Reflections

1. God is getting ready to do a new thing in your life. He's getting ready to deliver something amazing through you, but you got to be willing to give the final push. Is there anything you can think of that you wanted to do, but you feel as though its to late? What valid reason can you give for not forward?

2. In Genesis 32:24, Jacob was left alone; and there wrestled an angel with him until the breaking of the day. That thing that you desire from God is worth the wait. Are you willing to wrestle with Him? Are you willing to hold on to Him after the blessing?

ROUND 01
TODAY THE GIANT FALLS

If you only knew that God was setting you up for greatness. If you only knew that every attack in your life was strategically sent to elevate you, you would come out of your comfort zones, take your potion, starting right now. This was David's reality. We all had those moments when something began to come toward us and we believed that it was too much to handle. It was in that moment that fear kicked in and we didn't realize that with the right amount of faith, which is the size of a mustard seed, we could accomplish any task at hand. Question, how is big is your faith? In this life you will face some giants, don't try to escape them, don't try to avoid them, face them. I promise you, if you know who you are and whose you are, the battle is already over. Hey, what you decide to do when giants show up will show you who you are. We all face giants. It doesn't matter if you're black or white, whether you are rich or poor, educated or uneducated, saved or lost, all of us will face giants in life. You can be minding your own business and the giant will show up. They will show up because we serve a big God, they will show up because we serve a great God, they will show up because we serve a moving God, and because God is a moving God, He knows how to move things out of our way. In order for us to get to the next level, there are some transitions in life, some transformations in life, some transfigurations in life that are not accidents, but intents of

God to culminate in us, circumstances to confirm us, when everybody else refuses to believe that we can't. What God has done in my past no matter what other people say I can't do, I know what God can do. And because of what He has done, I can open my mouth and declare that God has prepared me for this moment, this test, this trial, this shift. Tell the enemy to get out of your way because you are coming through.

In fact, when we look through the Bible we see how God uses the most unqualified, the most unfavorable, to get things done. Peter was just a fisherman; Esther was just a girl who found favor in the king's sight. Naomi goes to Bethlehem and Ruth follows her. There Ruth meets Boaz, and from that union Obed is born. Obed has Jesse and Jesse has eight sons and David is the youngest.

Little David the shepherd boy, have you heard about him, anointed at the age of 15 but had to wait to occupy as King at age 30. God might set you up by the anointing, the arrangement, the announcement, but you have to go through some stuff for the appointment.

David knew he was anointed, and he wasn't trying to wait for the assignment. Just because you have mastered your poems, your skills, your victories over lions, tigers, and bears, oh my. On the mountain top, don't mean that you are in control, thank God for small assignments, small tasks, little victories, because they are building blocks God uses to build your character. Saul had a comeback for why he should remain king, but Saul didn't have a fightback when an uncircumcised Philistine showed up to his house. If you are going to be used by God, you are going to have to learn how to handle stuff that just shows up at your house.

Sickness will show up, relationship issues will show up, be late on your car note and the repo man will show up. Can I give you more? What's on your credit report will show up, when folks get tired of abuse something is going to show up.

Three of the oldest brothers are gone off to fight, but the real fight, is not happening on the battle field, the real fight happens at the house. A lion or bear shows up and takes a lamb, but a little boy name David rips the lion's beard, strikes it with his hand or a stick. The Bible says that the devil walketh about like roaring lion seeking whom he can devour, but when he showed up for the attack just like David, Jesus showed up and defeated him with a big stick, the cross.

We see that there is a problem that has touched down near the armies of Israel. Goliath shouted at them, he made fun of them, he wagged his tale at them, he kept coming with his insults against them, but he did not know that these were not the servants of Saul, these were the servants of God.

When God gets ready for you to go to the next level in life He will send you on a mission, an assignment. For David, his assignment was not to be commander, it was not to be king, it was a journey to position him for his shift in life. When we let the Lord choose our assignments, He will also give direction and battle strategies too. When this happens, something ordinary will become extraordinary because something great happens when we move for our Father.

You can be a young man or a young girl and know how to handle your giant. Somebody said something about your friend but instead of running to your friend and saying something, you looked out for them and spoke up yourself because you knew what to do with that giant. David said I might be less than enough, but with God I am more than enough to handle what comes my way. David is saying don't get caught up with looking at the kid in me that you can't see the king in me. Instead of looking at my frailty, take a look at my Father, and by Him, for Him, and through Him, I can do all things.

David knew that his destiny was not tied to what folks thought about him. David's oldest brother Eliab said I know why you are here. Eliab clearly doesn't know his younger brother. Instead of saying I know you think you all that, he should've said to the army of Israel "here comes your champion", but it's hard to vouch for folks in whom you never placed your confidence.

As David had answered his brother's passion with meekness, so David answered Saul's fear with faith. When David kept sheep, he proved himself very careful and tender of his flock. This reminds us of Christ, the good Shepherd, who not only ventured, but laid down his life for the sheep. This is the one God chose for this giant assignment, and like David, Jesus was chosen to fight our battles.

David knew how to take men who were not gifted enough but were found more than enough to handle the Philistines who rose up against his people.

When you decide to fight, make sure you have something in your hand. You need provision in your hand, you need promise in your hand. You need the Word of God in your hand. A few smooth stones are good too. In your hand, is your past. Use what you did in the past to get you into your future.

When you have God, every giant in your life will fall. Why? Because no giant in your physical life, or your spiritual life can stand against the Creator of the universe. Before the foundation of the world we have a champion and He is Lord. Just like the giant was cast out of heaven by the Rock of Ages, so did Goliath by the Spirit (wind) and the smooth rock or stone which is the Lord.

The Bible says that David takes his staff in his hand, he also choose five smooth stones from the brook, and puts them in his shepherds' bag, a pouch, and a sling was in his hand. When Goliath and David drew near Goliath made jokes and said, am I a little dog that you come at me with sticks? What Goliath didn't know was that the stick was just a disguise. I see the plan of salvation in this fight.

And the Philistine said to David, "Come to me, and I will give your flesh to the birds of the air and the beasts of the field!" Then David said to the Philistine, "You come to me with a sword, with a spear, and with a javelin. But I come to you in the name of the Lord of hosts, the God of the armies of Israel, whom you have defied. This day the Lord will deliver you into my hand, and I will strike you and take your head from you.
1 Samuel 17: 44-46

Goliath was not David's problem; He was David's promise.

The same thing David told Goliath in the field, is the same thing Jesus told the serpent in the garden.

Like David winded the sling up, for three years Jesus' ministry on earth was wound up. And when Jesus got through winding His ministry up, the giant was going to go down. The same thing Jesus showed the devil while hanging there on the cross, is the same thing Jesus want you to know right now.

***Today, your giant will fall.*ABCD**

When you got God, every giant in your life will fall. Why? Because no giant in your physical life, or your spiritual life can stand against the creator of the universe.

Reflections

-Make a list of every giant that needs to be destroyed in your life!

ROUND ①②
WE WILL WIN

Sometimes we lose because we find ourselves wrestling against things that are too great for us. It's like wrestling on the wrong level. It's like me going into the ring with the Ultimate Warrior, the Big Show, or John Cena. There are some things that come against us that are not right for us on so many levels. No matter the level, God is still greater. When we recognize who is on our side, we will discover that it's in that moment, the source of Gods strength is always greater than the power of our opponent.

In the movie Color Purple, Sofia said, "All my life I had to fight. I had to fight my daddy. I had to fight my uncles. I had to fight my brothers. A girl child aint safe in a family of men's, but I aint never thought I'd have to fight in my own house!! I loves Harpo, God knows I do. But I'll kill him dead 'fo I let him beat me."

I done had enough. Today you got the right one. Reasoning and talking about it has just left the building. This was not the case with Jehoshaphat, there was a whole city getting ready to come knock down his door. This is the Bible. This is better than HBO, and Cinemax. There is about to be a shake down. Grand mamas have showed up for this fight. Jehoshaphat knows he is in trouble. I'm here to let you know that when you're in trouble, the safest place in the whole wide world is in the will of God.

2 Chronicles 20 English Standard Version (ESV)
Jehoshaphat's Prayer.

After this the Moabites and Ammonites, and with them some of the Meunites,[a] came against Jehoshaphat for battle. Some men came and told Jehoshaphat, "A great multitude is coming against you from Edom,[b] from beyond the sea; and, behold, they are in Hazazon-tamar" (that is, Engedi). Then Jehoshaphat was afraid and set his face to seek the Lord, and proclaimed a fast throughout all Judah. And Judah assembled to seek help from the Lord; from all the cities of Judah they came to seek the Lord. And Jehoshaphat stood in the assembly of Judah and Jerusalem, in the house of the Lord, before the new court, and said, "O Lord, God of our fathers, are you not God in heaven? You rule over all the kingdoms of the nations. In your hand are power and might, so that none is able to withstand you. Did you not, our God, drive out the inhabitants of this land before your people Israel, and give it forever to the descendants of Abraham your friend? And they have lived in it and have built for you in it a sanctuary for your name, saying, And he said, "Listen, all Judah and inhabitants of Jerusalem and King Jehoshaphat: Thus says the Lord to you, 'Do not be afraid and do not be dismayed at this great horde, for the battle is not yours but God's. Tomorrow go down against them. Behold, they will come up by the ascent of Ziz. You will find them at the end of the valley, east of the wilderness of Jeruel. You will not need to fight in this battle. Stand firm, hold your position, and see the salvation of the Lord on your behalf, O Judah and Jerusalem.' Do not be afraid and do not be dismayed. Tomorrow go out against them, and the Lord will be with you."

2 Chronicles 20

Jehoshaphat, why are these people coming at you like this. Maybe he said something about somebody's mama. No, that can't be it because the Bible does not say that a family is coming after him, it says the multitude (a whole city, several of them). What Happened? Previously, in 2 Chronicles 18 Jehoshaphat teamed up with King Ahab in a fight against Ramoth Gilead. Jehoshaphat speaks to Ahab and said, "My people are your people, we family." I got you. Let's face it. There are some battles that need to be fought one on one. There are some battles that need none of your help. Maybe Jehoshaphat should have taken a ringside seat. Some battles only need your support, not your winning strategy. King Ahab took counsel and listened to 400 men rather than listening to the prophet who tried to give him warning that this battle was not going to fall in his favor. In 1 Kings 22:22, "The Holy Spirit said, I will be a lying Spirit in the mouth of men who speak for God."

The problem that Jehoshaphat is having in the text is because he has learned his lesson and turned to God. He has changed his life and now that he is doing great things and connected to God, trouble rises against him. Trouble has come back to haunt Jehoshaphat. He does not know it, but there are three separate armies sneaking up on him from behind, from a different route. He does not have time to develop a strategy. He does not even have time to remember what he had done to have this attack come against him. If it was today's time, somebody could've sent him a text, or went live on Facebook to say "Bro, they coming." Jehoshaphat did not send for this fight nor request it. The fight made way to his doorstep, free of charge!

Jehoshaphat begins to ask God some questions? Now that he is about to be attacked. And Jehoshaphat stood in the assembly of Judah and Jerusalem, in the house of the Lord, before the new court, and said, "O Lord, God of our fathers, are you not God in heaven? You rule over all the kingdoms of the nations. In your hand are power and might, so that none is able to withstand you."

Just like Jehoshaphat, God wants you to stand firm and hold your position. What position God? We have no training. We are not men and women of war. We do not know Ty Kwando or Jujitsu. Listen, the position that the Lord is talking about is a position and posture of prayer. There is power in prayer and fasting. Sing praises to God. Jehoshaphat knew that his peace was his responsibility so he looked to God.

When the enemy comes against you, when your money start acting funny, when that assignment sneaks up on you, when its almost time to go back to school and your mama haven't bought you your new shoes yet, start praising God's name. Praise is what confuses the enemy. While everybody thought that you would be mad and bent out of shape, stressed, and perplexed, because of what came against you, thought that you were just going to cry and throw yourself on the floor and die, instead they see you happy. Know now that every attack against you was only sent to maneuver you where God wants you to be.

There is nothing like good examples. Jesus is our example. Some people will advise you without knowing the nature of your challenges and expect that what worked for them, is going to work for you. That's not always the case. Ahab died in his battle. Ahab inquiring of men whether or not he would win the battle should've informed him that the battle was not his, but he chose to fight and wrestle on the wrong level. Have you been handling your situations in your own strength? Have you given up on the very source that has the answer for your problem? If so, just know right now that the battle is not yours it's the Lord's. I believe that we will win. The battle is the Lord's!

God wants you to stand firm and hold your position. There is power in prayer.

SUMMARY AND CONCLUSION

In my early school days, I had a teacher who was just hard on me. At least that is what I thought. She made it difficult for me and would often speak in harsh tones. I had been written up often in this class even when I thought I was on my best behavior. I would do my best but my best was only as good as her affirmation for me to achieve in the class. When I began to matriculate at a junior college, guess who my math teacher was? Yup, the same elementary teacher. Oh boy. I failed the class twice with a "D" not because I could not understand the work, but because of what I held against her from what I experienced earlier in grade school, prejudice, etc. I could've requested for another class but at the time I was just glad to be in college. I had to pass this class. I took it again, but this time with another teacher and she was very good. Her name was Ms. Woods. I told Ms. Woods at the beginning of the semester that I was going to pass the class with nothing less than a "B." Why not an "A?"

I had an "A" in this class pretty much all the way through. I had an opportunity to make a 100 on my final exam, but I missed about 3 questions on purpose because I had believed that if I made a 100 on the final exam and received a letter grade of 100 on my report card, that the administration would have believed I cheated. Crazy thinking, I know, but I was so worried about being average and what people thought I couldn't do, that I psychologically thought that the best thing for me to do was live only up to the expectation of what they thought. Instead of getting a 100 on my report card I settled to receive something less. My teacher told me that I could achieve and make whatever grade I chose. She provided the instruction and made way for me to pass and be confident while doing it. For me it was a lesson learned.

Truth is, many people operate by what others think about them. Who cares what they think! God has destined you for greatness, and guess what, no matter what other people think go ahead and get your "A."

Listen to me closely.

Don't let other people's rejection of you eradicate, exterminate, and eliminate what God is about to do in your life. Go on and be great.

It is often stated that revolution has always come out of a fight, but if the truth be told, many have taken themselves out of the fight because they are so afraid to lose, and never realizing that it was necessary to lose. The loss was set up by God to hand you something greater. What's great is your history. What's great is your deliverance. What's great is your destiny. What's great is the comeback from the setback of societies disapproval of your ability to win. You are special and are chosen by God and destined for greatness. Go tell somebody this is how we fight our battles!

ABOUT THE AUTHOR

Nickalos Baker is a pastor, motivational speaker, and gifted singer. He has a passion for social justice and helping people identify their purpose, even during tough times. Spreading the love through the Gospel of Jesus is his aim. He currently pastors three churches, Ephesus SDA TN, Cottage Chapel SDA KY, First Love SDA KY. Nickalos is married to Tabatha Baker, and they have three beautiful children and live in Clarksville, TN. He believes that great things never come from comfort zones and admonishes us all to get in the fight.